CHAPMAN
NAUTICAL
CHART No. 1

CHAPMAN
NAUTICAL
CHART No. 1

UNITED STATES
COAST GUARD

The Essential Guide
to Chart Reading
and Navigation

HEARST BOOKS

A Division of Sterling Publishing Co., Inc
New York

Book design by Howard R. Roberts, HRoberts Design
Cover Design by Celia Fuller

Library of Congress Cataloging-in-Publication Data
United States. Coast Guard.
  Chapman nautical chart no. 1 : the essential guide to chart reading and naviga-
tion / United States Coast Guard & John Wooldridge.
     p. cm.
  Includes index.
  ISBN 1-58816-400-4
  1. Navigation. 2. Nautical charts. I. Wooldridge, John, 1947- II. Title.
  VK559.U54 2004
  623.89'22--dc22
                                                                        2004009407

10 9 8 7 6 5 4 3 2 1

Published by Hearst Books
A Division of Sterling Publishing Co., Inc.
387 Park Avenue South, New York, N.Y. 10016

**Includes complete text of *Chart No. 1 Nautical Chart Symbols, Abbreviations
and Terms*; published by the Government Printing Office.**

Distributed in Canada by Sterling Publishing
c/o Canadian Manda Group, 165 Dufferin Street
Toronto, Ontario, Canada M6K 3H6

Printed in China

ISBN 1-58816-400-4

Contents

Introduction

Within its 12-mile territorial borders and 200-mile fisheries jurisdiction, there are approximately 3.5 million square nautical miles of navigable U.S. waters and more than 95,000 miles of coastline that boat operators must contend with. Nautical charts and other information sources produced by the National Oceanic and Atmospheric Administration (NOAA) and its divisions promote safe and efficient navigation of these waters for a wide variety of users, including recreational boaters, state and local governments, the U.S. Department of Defense and commercial shipping and fishing industries.

A nautical chart is a detailed picture of the marine environment: a watery road map loaded with vital information. More than that, it's a fundamental tool, a working document that is essential for safe navigation. Leaving the dock without a current chart of local waters, especially waters that you know like the back of your hand, can be risky in the extreme. In conjunction with supplemental fixed, floating, and electronic navigational aids, a chart lets you lay out courses and navigate your vessel by the shortest route through safe waters.

A chart shows, among other things, the shape, natures and form of the coast; the depths of the water; and general characteristics of the sea bottom. It also pinpoints dangers to navigation and the locations of man-made aids to navigation, and indicates the local magnetic characteristics that will affect your compass readings. A chart contains supplemental information ranging from tide heights to pictures of dangerous areas such as cable or pipeline crossings.

But the range of information depicted on charts is voluminous, much more than can be referenced in the land-mass margins. This book reprints "Chart No. 1—Nautical Chart Symbols Abbreviations and Terms," a comprehensive reference publication containing the basic chart elements and symbols used on the NOAA's Coast Survey charts as well as those of many other nations. This book also reprints portions of two chapters of the 64th edition of *Chapman Piloting & Seamanship.*

According to the NOAA, about 3,500 ships are involved in accidents on our nation's waterways, in addition to the approximately 6,400 recreational boating accidents that are reported annually. Our intent is to supplement your understanding of charts and charting to ensure safer boating.

— Capt. John Wooldridge

I

The Nautical Chart

BASIC CHART CONCEPTS

To travel anywhere safely in his boat, a skipper must have knowledge of water depths, shoals, and channels. The location of aids to navigation and landmarks must be known, as well as ports and harbors. At any given position, depth can usually be measured and some landmarks seen, but for true safety, a boater has to know the depth ahead, the actual location of the aids to navigation seen, and where more aids lie on the course that will be followed. To plan the best route to his destination, he must know the dangers to navigation along the way. This information can best be determined from up-to-date nautical charts. Not only must the skipper have the required charts on board, he or she must know how to use them.

CHARTS VS. MAPS

A MAP is a representation in miniature—usually to some proportional scale—on a plane surface, of a portion of the earth's surface for use on land. In it the emphasis is on roads, cities, and political boundaries; see **Figure I-1**.

A NAUTICAL CHART is a similar representation in miniature—to scale—emphasizing the water areas and natural and man-made features of particular interest to a navigator; see **Figure I-2**.

A chart includes information about depth of water, obstructions and other hazards to navigation, and the location and type of aids to navigation. Adjacent land areas are portrayed only with details

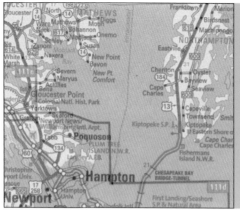

Figure I-1 *A map is designed to emphasize information about land features such as roads—as shown here on this map of the lower Chesapeake Bay area of the Atlantic Coast. Underwater and coastal features are almost ignored.*

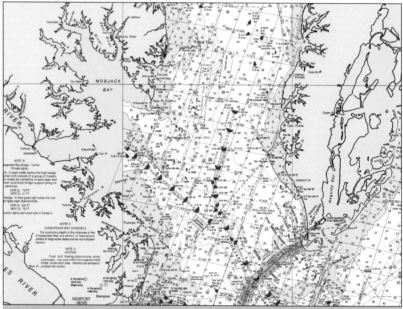

Figure I-2 *A nautical chart of Chesapeake Bay is far more detailed than a map of the same area. It is almost exclusively concerned with navigation on the water. Note the amount of data that is conveyed by each square inch of the chart—all achieved without compromising its clarity.*

that aid a navigator—the shoreline, harbor facilities, and prominent natural or man-made features. Charts are printed on heavyweight, durable paper so that they may be used as worksheets on which courses may be plotted and positions determined. For skippers of small craft, there are even special charts showing details on marinas and similar facilities.

A chart's basic purpose is to give the navigator information that enables him to make the *right decision in time to avoid danger*. Charts differ from road maps both in kinds of information and in the precision of their details: for safety, charts must be extremely accurate. Even a small error in charting the position of a submerged obstruction can be a serious hazard to navigation.

Various "cruising guides" are available for many boating areas. These are useful for planning a nautical trip and include chart reproductions or extracts, textual information, useful data, and even aerial photographs. What these lack, however, are provisions for revisions between printings comparable to *Notices to Mariners'* changes for official charts. So take advantage of the information available in cruising guides, but do *not* try to substitute them for genuine nautical charts.

GEOGRAPHIC COORDINATES

Charts show a grid of intersecting lines to aid in describing a specific position on the water. These lines are charted representations of a system of GEOGRAPHIC COORDINATES that are imagined to exist on the earth's surface.

The earth is nearly spherical in shape—it is slightly flattened along the polar axis, but the distortion is minimal and need concern only those who construct the charts, not boaters. A GREAT CIRCLE is the line traced out on the surface of a sphere by a plane cutting through the sphere at its center; see **Figure I-3**, upper. It is the largest circle that can be drawn on the surface of a sphere. A SMALL CIRCLE is one marked on the surface of a sphere by a plane that does not pass through its center; see **Figure I-3**, lower.

Meridians and Parallels

Geographic coordinates are defined by two sets of great and small circles. One is a set of great circles, each of which passes through the north and south geographic poles—these are the MERIDIANS OF LONGITUDE; see **Figure I-4**, left. The other set is a series of circles each established by a plane cutting through the earth perpendicular

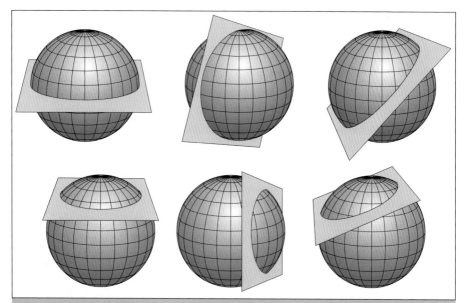

Figure I-3 *A great circle, top, is the line traced on the surface of sphere by a plane that cuts through the center of the sphere. A small circle, bottom, is a line traced on the surface of a sphere that does not cut through the sphere's center.*

to the polar axis. The largest of these is midway between the poles and thus passes through the center of the earth, becoming a great circle; this is the EQUATOR. Other parallel planes from small circles are known as the PARALLELS OF LATITUDE; see Figure **I-4**, right.

Geographic coordinates are measured in terms of DEGREES (one degree is 1/360th of a complete circle). The meridian that passes through Greenwich, England is the reference for all measurements of longitude and is designated as the PRIME MERIDIAN, or 0°. The longitude of any position on earth is described as so many degrees East or West of Greenwich, to a maximum in either direction of 180°. The measurement can be thought of as either the angle at the North and South Poles between the meridian of the place being described and the prime meridian, or as the arc along the equator between these meridians; see **Figure I-5**, left. The designation of "E" or "W" is an essential part of any statement of longitude, abbreviated as "Long," "Lo," or "λ" (the Greek letter *lambda*).

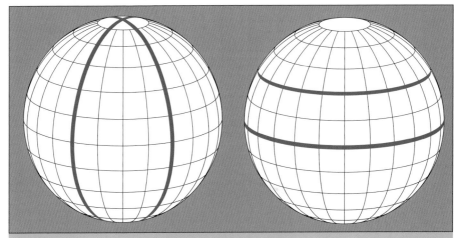

Figure I-4 *Meridians of longitude on the earth are great circles, left, that pass through both the North and South Poles. Parallels of latitude, right, are small circles that are parallel to the plane of the Equator. The Equator is a great circle that is perpendicular to the earth's axis.*

Parallels of latitude are measured in degrees north or south from the Equator, from 0° at the Equator to 90° at each pole. The designation of latitude (abbreviated as "Lat." or "L") must include "N" or "S" as necessary to provide a complete position; **see Figure I-5**, right.

For greater precision degrees are subdivided into MINUTES (60 minutes = 1 degree) and SECONDS (60 seconds = 1 minute). In some instances, minutes are divided decimally, and for very high precision, seconds can be so divided.

From **Figure I-5**, left, you can see that the meridians of longitude get closer together as one moves away from the Equator in either direction, and converge at the poles. Thus, the *distance* on the earth's surface between adjacent meridians is not a fixed quantity but varies with latitude. On the other hand, except for extremely small technicalities, the parallels of latitude are equally spaced, and the distance between successive parallels is the same. One degree of latitude is, for all practical purposes, 60 nautical miles; *one minute of latitude is used as one nautical mile*, a relationship that we will later see is quite useful.

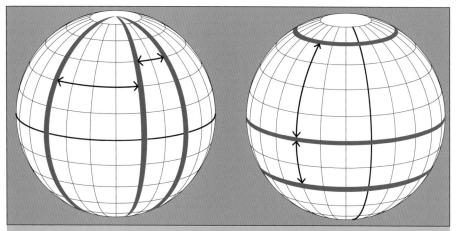

Figure I-5 *Longitude, left, is measured from the prime meridian (0°), which passes through Greenwich, England, east or west to a maximum of 180°. Latitude, right, is measured north or south from the equator (0°) to the poles (90°). Meridians of longitude and parallels of latitude are shown at 15° intervals.*

CHART CONSTRUCTION

The construction of a chart tries to solve the problem of representing a spherical, three-dimensional surface on a plane—a two-dimensional sheet of paper. It is actually impossible to accomplish this exactly, and a certain amount of distortion is inevitable, but various methods, called PROJECTIONS, do provide practical and sufficiently accurate results.

The transfer of information from the sphere to the chart's flat surface should be accomplished with as little distortion as possible to both the shape and the size of land and water areas, the angular relation of positions, the distance between points, and other more technical properties. Each projection is superior in one or more of these qualities; none is superior in all characteristics. In all projections, as the area covered by the chart is decreased, the distortion diminishes, and the difference among types of projections lessens.

Of the many projection techniques that are used, two are of primary interest to boaters. The MERCATOR PROJECTION is an example of the most common; it is used for charts of ocean and coastal areas. The POLYCONIC PROJECTION is employed for National Ocean Service (NOS) charts of the Great Lakes and some inland rivers. The average skipper can quite safely navigate his boat using either type of chart without a deep knowledge of the techniques of projection.

DIRECTION

DIRECTION is defined as the angle between a line connecting one point with another, and a base, or reference, line such as the geographic or magnetic meridian passing through the original point; the angle is measured in degrees clockwise from the reference line. Thus, direction on charts may be described as so many degrees TRUE (T) or so many degrees MAGNETIC (M). The difference between these directions is VARIATION and must be allowed for, as described in Chapter 13. The principal difference in the use of charts on the Mercator projection from those on the polyconic projection lies in the techniques for measuring direction.

Measurement of Direction

To facilitate the measurement of direction, as in plotting bearings and laying out courses, most charts have COMPASS ROSES printed on them. A compass rose consists of two or three concentric circles, several inches in diameter and accurately subdivided; see **Figure I-6**. The outer circle has its zero at *True* North; this is emphasized with a star. The next circle or circles are oriented to *magnetic* North. The next inner circle is magnetic direction expressed in degrees, with an arrow printed over the zero point to indicate magnetic North. The innermost circle, if there are three, also represents magnetic direction, but in terms of "points," and halves and quarters thereof; its use by modern boaters is limited. (One point = 11¼ degrees).

The difference between the orientation of the two outer sets of circles is the magnetic variation at the location of the compass rose. The amount of the variation and its direction (easterly or westerly) is given in words and figures in the center of the rose, together with a statement of the year that such variation existed and the annual rate of change. When using a chart in a year much later than the compass rose date, it *may* be necessary to modify the variation shown by applying the annual rate of change. Such cases are relatively rare

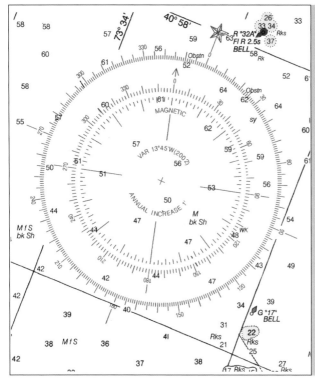

Figure I-6 *A compass rose illustrates True North and magnetic North. The outer circle is calibrated in degrees, with zero at true north. The inner circles are in degrees and "points," with their zero at magnetic north. Several compass roses are located on each chart at locations convenient for plotting course and bearings. Some charts of the Small Craft series omit the innermost circle with its point system of subdivision.*

because rates are quite small, and differences of a fraction of a degree may generally be ignored. Each chart has several compass roses printed on it in locations that do not conflict with navigational information.

Until a skipper has thoroughly mastered the handling of compass "errors," he should use only true directions and the true (outer) compass rose. Later, the magnetic rose may be used *directly*, thus simplifying computations.

Several cautions are necessary when measuring directions on charts. For large-area charts, the magnetic variation can differ for various portions of the chart. Check each chart when you first start to use it, and, to be sure, always use the compass rose *nearest* the area for which you are plotting. Depending upon a chart's type and scale, graduations on its compass rose circles may be for intervals of 1°, 2°, or 5°. On some charts, the outer (True North) is subdivided into units of 1° while the inner (Magnetic North) circle, being smaller, is subdivided into steps of 2°. Always check to determine the interval between adjacent marks on each compass rose scale.

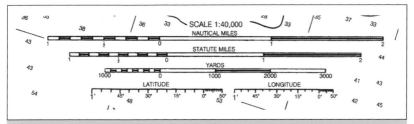

Figure I-7 *NOS charts of scales of 1:80,000 and larger will have one scale of nautical miles and one of yards; those for the Great Lakes, inland rivers, and the Intracoastal Waterways will also carry a scale of statute miles. This 1:40,000 small-craft chart additionally has latitude and longitude scales showing subdivisions of one minute.*

DISTANCE

DISTANCES on charts are measured in statute or nautical miles. Use of the STATUTE (LAND) MILE of 5,280 feet (approximately 1,609 m) is limited to the Great Lakes, inland rivers, and the Atlantic and Gulf Intracoastal Waterways. The NAUTICAL MILE of 6,076.1 feet (exactly 1,852 m) is used on ocean and coastal waters.

In navigation, distances of up to a mile or so usually are expressed in YARDS, a unit that is the same no matter which "mile" is used on the chart. Foreign charts will commonly use METERS for shorter distances, and this unit may come into wider use on U.S. charts.

Conversion factors and rules of thumb are shown in the accompanying Unit Conversion box.

Conversions can also be made graphically using graphic bar scales; see **Figure I-7**. A distance measured on one scale by using a pair of dividers can be measured on another scale to determine the equivalent distance.

CHART SCALES

The amount by which actual distances are reduced for representation on a chart is known as the SCALE of that chart; many different scales are used. Scale may be expressed as a ratio, 1:80,000 meaning

UNIT CONVERSION

On salt water, distances are measured in nautical miles, whereas the statute mile is used on shore, in fresh water bodies, and along the Intracoastal Waterways (ICWs). Depths are usually measured in feet on inshore and near-coastal waters; offshore, the unit of depth measurement is the fathom—which is 6 feet (1.83 m). Increasingly, metric units are coming into use for guaging depths and short distances.

While it is easy to make conversions graphically by using the various unit scales presented, you may also need to make conversions by using the numeric conversion factors given below (factors are rounded, except where shown as "exactly"), or by using quick rules of thumb, as shown at bottom.

- nautical miles x 1.15 = statute miles
- statute miles x 0.87 = nautical miles
- nautical miles x 1,852 = meters (exactly)
- meters x 0.00054 = nautical miles
- nautical miles x 2,025.4 = yards
- yards x 0.00049 = nautical miles
- statute miles x 1,609 = meters
- meters x 0.00062 = statute miles
- statute miles x 1,760 = yards (exactly)
- yards x 0.9144 = meters
- meters x 1.094 = yards
- fathoms x 6 = feet
- feet x 0.16667 = fathoms
- fathoms x 1.828 = meters
- meters x 0.5468 = fathoms

Rules of Thumb

Roughly 7 nautical miles equals 8 statute miles, so you can convert nautical to statute by multiplying nautical miles by 8 and dividing the product by 7. To reverse the conversion: statute miles times 7, then divide by 8. A nautical mile has about 2,000 yards—close enough for quick calculations.

that 1 unit on the chart represents 80,000 units on the actual land or water surface, or as a fraction (1/80,000) with the same meaning. This is termed the NATURAL SCALE of the chart.

The ratio of chart to actual distance can also be expressed as a NUMERICAL or EQUIVALENT SCALE, such as "1 inch = 1.1 miles,"—another way of expressing a 1:80,000 scale. Equivalent scales are not as commonly used on nautical charts as on maps, but they may be encountered in publications such as cruising guides.

Charts at a scale of 1:80,000 or larger (e.g., 1:40,000) will normally carry, in addition to a statement of scale, two sets of graphic bar scales, each subdivided into conveniently and commonly used units; refer to **Figure I-7**. Note that one basic unit is placed to the *left* of the scale's zero point and is subdivided more finely than is the main part of the scale. The use of these graphic scales is covered in Chapter 16.

When using Mercator charts, the navigator can take advantage of the fact that one minute on the *latitude* scale on each *side* of the chart is essentially equal to one nautical mile. (Do *not* use the longitude scale at the top or bottom of the chart.) On charts of a scale 1:80,000 and smaller (e.g., 1:1,200,000) the latitude scale will be the only means of measuring distance.

It is important to fix in your mind the scale of the chart you are using, lest you misjudge distances. Quite often in a day's cruise you may use charts of different scales, changing back and forth between small-scale coastal charts and larger-scale harbor charts. Unless you are aware of the differing scales, you may find yourself in a dangerous position.

A LOGARITHMIC SPEED SCALE is printed on all charts of 1:40,000 or larger scale; see **Figure I-8**. It is useful for graphically solving problems of time, speed, and distance.

CHART SOURCES

Charts are prepared and issued by several agencies of the U.S. federal government. This is not duplication, however, because different agencies are responsible for different areas and types of

Figure I-8 *NOS charts of 1:40,000 or larger scale carry a Logarithmic Speed Scale that can be used to graphically solve problems of time, distance, and speed.*

charts. Most boaters use charts prepared by the National Ocean Service (NOS) of the National Oceanic and Atmospheric Administration, (NOAA) U.S. Department of Commerce. NOS charts (sometimes referred to as NOAA charts) cover the Great Lakes and the coastal waters of the United States, including harbors and rivers extending inland to the head of tidal action.

The National Imagery and Mapping Agency (NIMA) publishes charts of the high seas and foreign waters based on its own and other nations' surveys. (Some of these charts may still bear the name of the former publishing agency: the Defense Mapping Agency Hydrographic/Topographic Center, or DMAHTC.) Boaters will use NIMA charts, for example, when cruising in the Bahamas.

Charts of major inland rivers such as the Mississippi and Ohio are issued by the U.S. Army Corps of Engineers. Also available are charts of many inland lakes and canal systems.

Canadian waters are charted by the Canadian Hydrographic Service, an agency of that country's Department of Fisheries and Oceans.

LARGE SCALE and SMALL SCALE

When chart scales are expressed fractionally, confusion sometimes results from the use of the terms "large scale" and "small scale." Since the number that is varied to change the scale is the denominator of the fraction, as it gets larger, the fraction, and hence the scale, gets smaller. For example, 1/80,000 is a smaller fraction than 1/40,000, so a chart to the former scale is termed a smaller-scale chart.

The terms "large scale" and "small scale" are relative and have no limiting definitions. Scales may be as large as 1:5,000 for detailed harbor charts, or as small as 1 to several million for charts of large areas of the world.

Chart Catalogs

The catalogs from issuing agencies indicate the area covered by each chart, the scale used, the price, and the type of radionavigation system (Loran) charted, if any. These catalogs are useful for planning a cruise into unfamiliar waters.

The National Ocean Service publishes four free chart catalogs;

- Atlantic and Gulf Coasts, including Puerto Rico and the Virgin Islands
- Pacific Coast, including Hawaii, Mariana, and Samoa Islands
- Alaska, including the Aleutian Islands
- Great Lakes and Adjacent Waterways.

These catalogs are actually small-scale outline charts with diagrams delineating the areas covered by each NOS chart. They are also sources of information on other NOS publications and charts, as well as publications of other agencies; in additon they contain a listing, organized by state, of the names and addresses of local sales agents for nautical charts and other publications.

The *NIMA Catalog, Part 2, Volume—Nautical Charts and Publications* is available as nine individual catalogs covering international waters including the U.S and Canada. The catalogs are free of charge and available from your local NOS chart sales agent or may be ordered from the NOS Distribution Branch.

NOS Offices

For information about National Ocean Service charts, publications and activities, write, phone, fax, or send e-mail to:

Director, Office of Coast Survey
SSMC-3, Room 6147
1315 East-West Highway
Silver Spring, MD 20910-3282
Phone: 1-301-713-2770
Fax: 1-301-713-4019
www.chartmaker.ncd.noaa.gov

Regional Marine Centers are located at Norfolk, Virginia, and Seattle, Washington.

Where to Buy Charts

Charts may be purchased directly from the headquarters or field offices of the issuing agencies, or from retail sales agents. The addresses of NOS and NIMA distribution offices are given in Appendix A. Sales agents are widely located in boating and shipping centers. The names and addresses of local sales agents for NOS charts and publications are listed in the various chart catalogs. These lists are footnoted to indicate agents also stocking NIMA charts and USCG publications. Each volume of the NIMA chart catalogs lists sales agents, including those in foreign countries.

The price of NOS and DMAHTC charts has risen significantly in recent years and continues to rise nearly every year. For many boating areas, the cost of a full set has become a major expense for a boater. These greater prices, however, still do not cover the full costs of surveys, data compilation, printing, and distribution. Even so, government charts are still a bargain considering the extent, accuracy, and importance of the information that they provide.

A discount is allowed to each local sales agent for quantity purchases. It is also possible for a boat or yacht club or other boating organization to purchase charts in bulk for a discount.

Reproductions of government charts are also available from commercial organizations in bound volumes for greater convenience and at somewhat lower cost.

You should keep a full set of charts aboard for the waters you cruise, and regularly replace worn-out or outdated charts with new ones. Failure to have a proper chart could be a factor in determining liability in the event of an accident.

PRINT-ON-DEMAND CHARTS

A recent development in nautical charting is the NOAA program of "Print-on-Demand" (POD). This is the use of large-format inkjet printers to produce charts at a decentralized location. Files are maintained in NOS databases and updated weekly with data that is published in *Notices to Mariners* and *Local Notices to Mariners,* as well as information from NOS field activities and cooperating organizations not yet published. Updated digital chart images are transmitted from NOS to the printing activity each hour. Here the actual printing is done only when an order is received by a retail agent and the chart is shipped for overnight delivery. The technology is not suitable for walk-in service or for implementation at all sales agencies.

Print-on-Demand offers the following benefits for users:

- Nautical charts that are up-to-date when they are purchased, instead of charts that may be many months, even years, old when sold. A new edition is available five to eight weeks before the conventionally printed chart is in the distribution system. Additionally, a user can go to the Internet site www.chartmaker.ncd.noaa.gov/pod and see the schedule for prospective new editions, thereby avoiding buying a chart that will soon be replaced.
- POD charts are even better than before—they feature brighter colors and higher contrast for improved readability in various light conditions. The paper used is water- and abrasion-resistant. Charts can be furnished in a double-sided laminated version for a small additional fee.
- Charts that are normally overprinted with Loran-C lines may now be ordered without such lines; this will result in charts with greater clarity for the many users who no longer use Loran as a navigation tool. (Some notes relating to Loran will not be removed and will remain on the face of the chart or in the margins.) A probable future development is the capability to print charts customized for a user's specialized needs, such as routes in water areas and additional features in land areas. Other products, such as reduced-scale "Pocket charts," are also being considered in this still-developing area of navigational aids.

Print-on-Demand provides the following benefits for sales agents and the government:

- Reduction of the need for space and the cost of maintaining inventories.
- Elimination of the wasteful obsolescence of charts when a new edition is issued.

Print-on-Demand charts are official and sufficient to meet all legal requirements where applicable. (Current editions of charts are not required on board recreational small craft, but their availability and use will be beneficial in case of accidents, lawsuits, etc.) POD charts carry the usual edition number and publication date, but also have an "Additional Corrections" box in the lower-left corner that notes the latest NIMA information data and *Local Notices to Mariners* for which the chart has been corrected.

There are, however, some disadvantages. Conventional POD charts are somewhat larger than the normally printed versions. This added space is put to good use with additional information, but the larger size may make handling more difficult on smaller boats. The NOS produces many charts as "small-craft editions" printed on both sides of lighter-weight paper and accordion-folded for ease of use in limited spaces. When prepared as Print-on-Demand charts, these are printed on one side of regular-weight paper with multiple parallel strips covering the various section of the route concerned—these are often even larger than conventional POD charts and could present quite a problem if used at the helm of smaller boats.

Nearly all NOS charts (98 percent as of early 2003) are now available in the Print-on-Demand format; information on availability can be found at the website mentioned above. These charts can be purchased from many of the larger chart sales agents—again, see the website for the current list of retail dealers. Charts that are ordered at one of these dealers (in person or by phone, fax, or Internet) will normally be available the next business day; they can be picked up at the store or drop-shipped directly to the user. (Occasionally, a retail agent may have in stock a POD chart that is up-to-date for all corrections.)

The cost of a POD chart is a few dollars more than a convention-ally printed chart. The POD system supplements, but does not replace, the long-standing chart distribution system and charts as we have known them for many years remain available.

POD Charts in Canada

The Canadian Hydrographic Service (CHS) also provides a print-on-demand chart service. There are some differences from the NOS operations, but the result is similar for users.

The information for many CHS charts is now stored in digital data-bases that are updated on a continuous basis from *Notices to Mariners;* CHS prints the charts in Ottawa using large-format inkjet printers. Charts not yet in the database are printed lithographically as before, and commercial charts continue to be hand-amended prior to being issued to dealers. A few charts of a specialized nature will con-tinue to be press-printed. Charts that are printed in the POD system are not available in the older printing-press format. For most of the year charts are printed only when an order from a dealer has been received. During the busy summer months, charts are printed ahead of time and in small batches based on anticipated demand.

With POD, CHS no longer needs to print large inventories of charts and hand-correct them with cumulative Notices to Mariners before distribution to dealers. For customers this means that charts are up to date as of the time they are printed by the CHS. POD allows CHS to issue charts to customers six to eight weeks faster and to have continual availability compared with press-printed charts.

Because these charts are up-to-date at the time of printing, cus-tomers no longer receive charts that contain hand-drawn amend-ments and ironed-on patches. The product is a fresh, clean, completely machine-drawn chart.

CHS POD charts are priced the same as the lithographically printed charts they replace.

Future plans being considered include expanding POD to the dealer level. CHS is currently conducting a POD test project at one dealer, evaluating both the technology and business case.

B
ANATOMY
OF A CHART

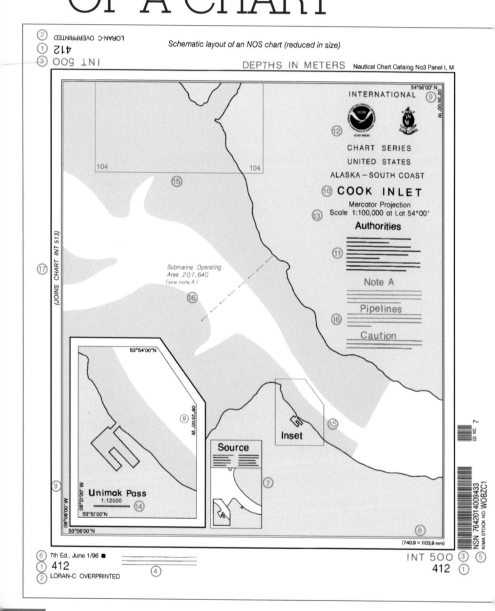

Schematic layout of an NOS chart (reduced in size)

DEPTHS IN METERS   Nautical Chart Catalog No3 Panel I, M

INTERNATIONAL

CHART SERIES
UNITED STATES
ALASKA – SOUTH COAST

COOK INLET
Mercator Projection
Scale 1:100,000 at Lat 54°00'

Authorities

Note A

Pipelines

Caution

Submarine Operating
Area 207.640
(see note A)

(JOINS CHART INT 513)

104

104

54°56'00" N

Inset

Source

Unimak Pass
1:12500

53°54'00"N

53°51'00"N

53°06'00"N

7th Ed., June 1/96
412
LORAN-C OVERPRINTED

INT 500
412

(740,9 × 1103,9 mm)

ED NO. 7

NSN 7642014009433
NIMA STOCK NO. WOBZC1

LORAN-C OVERPRINTED
412
INT 500

Chart number in national chart series
Identification of a latticed chart (if any): D for Decca   LC for Loran-C   Om for Omega
Chart number in international chart series (if any)
Publication note (imprint)
Bar Code and Stock Numbers
Edition note. In the example: Seventh edition published in June, 1996
Source data diagram (if any). For attention to navigators: use caution where surveys are inadequate
Dimensions of inner borders
Corner co-ordinates
Chart title } May be quoted when ordering a chart, in addition to chart number
Explanatory notes on chart construction, etc. To be read before using chart
Seals: In the example, the national and International Hydrographic Organization seals show that this national chart is also an international one. Purely national charts have the national seal only. Reproductions of charts of other nations (facsimile) have the seals of the original producer (left), publisher (center) and the IHO (right)
Projection and scale of chart at stated latitude. The scale is precisely as stated only at the latitude quoted
Linear scale on large-scale charts
Reference to a larger-scale chart
Cautionary notes (if any). Information on particular features, to be read before using chart
Reference to an adjoining chart of similar scale

C

HOW TO READ A CHART

WHAT CHARTS SHOW

Charts include much information that you should study thoroughly before you actually use them for navigation. Clear off the kitchen or dining room table and spread your charts out—do it before you cruise into any unfamiliar waters. Study charts can also be displayed on computers using chart-planning programs. This can provide a measure of "boating fun" when the weather is too cold or too wet and windy to get your craft under way. There is an amazing amount of information on every nautical chart; learn how to extract every bit of it.

When hydrographic surveys have been completed, cartographers are presented with vast amounts of information—so much so that if they were to include it all, charts would be a useless mass of black and colored ink. The cartographer's task is to edit the survey information: to make decisions as to what to include and what to leave out. Even so, such a large amount of data remains that every element on the printed chart must be made to carry meaning. To learn to read a chart, you must recognize that nothing without significance has been placed there.

BASIC INFORMATION

Located on the chart, where space is available, is the GENERAL INFORMATION or TITLE BLOCK; see **Figure I-9**. Here is the chart title describing the waters covered (the chart number does not appear here, but rather in several places around the margins);

Figure I-9 *The title block of a chart shows the official name of the chart, the type of projection, and scale, plus the datum and unit of measurement for depths. Printed nearby is much valuable information, so be sure to read all notes before using any chart.*

COAST SURVEY

UNITED STATES – WEST COAST

CALIFORNIA

SAN FRANCISCO BAY

ANGEL ISLAND TO POINT SAN PEDRO

Mercator Projection
Scale 1:20,000 at Lat. 37°55'
North American Datum of 1983
(World Geodetic System 1984)
SOUNDINGS IN FEET
AT MEAN LOWER LOW WATER

a statement of the type of projection used and the scale; the unit of depth measurement (feet or fathoms [one fathom equals six feet] or meters), and the datum plane for such soundings. (Caution: if the chart has INSETS—"blowups" of areas of special interest—these will be at a larger scale than the chart as a whole.)

Elsewhere on the chart, where space is available (normally in land areas), you will find other information: the meaning of certain commonly used abbreviations, units and the datum for heights above water, notes of caution regarding dangers, tidal information, references to anchorage areas, and a statement of the applicable volume of the *Coast Pilot*. Read *all* notes on charts because they provide important information that cannot be graphically presented; see **Figure I-10**.

Editions and Revisions

The edition number and publication date of a chart are at the lower left-hand corner; immediately following these figures is the date of the latest revised printing, if any. Under a policy adopted in late 2002, only the month and year of the chart's printing will be shown, and nearby will be separate information indicating the dates of the latest NIMA *Notice to Mariners* and USCG *Local Notice to Mariners* through which the chart has been corrected; see **Figure I-11**. These dates may be several weeks prior to the printing date due to

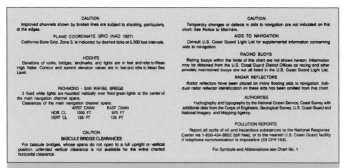

CAUTION	CAUTION
Improved channels shown by broken lines are subject to shoaling, particularly at the edges.	Temporary changes or defects in aids to navigation are not indicated on this chart. See Notice to Mariners.
PLANE COORDINATE GRID (NAD 1927)	**AIDS TO NAVIGATION**
California State Grid, Zone 3, is indicated by dashed ticks at 5,000 foot intervals.	Consult U.S. Coast Guard Light List for supplemental information concerning aids to navigation.
	RACING BUOYS
HEIGHTS	Racing buoys within the limits of this chart are not shown hereon. Information may be obtained from the U.S. Coast Guard District Offices as racing and other privately maintained buoys are not all listed in the U.S. Coast Guard Light List.
Elevations of rocks, bridges, landmarks, and lights are in feet and refer to Mean High Water. Contour and summit elevation values are in feet and refer to Mean Sea Level.	
	RADAR REFLECTORS
	Radar reflectors have been placed on many floating aids to navigation. Individual radar reflector identification on these aids has been omitted from this chart.

Figure I-10 *Notes printed on charts may concern navigation regulations, hazardous conditions at inlets, information on controlling depths that cannot be printed conveniently alongside a channel, or other matters that relate to navigation.*

Figure I-11 *The edition number and date, month, and year of printing of each NOS chart are printed in the margin, at the lower left-hand corner along with the chart number. Also shown are the dates of the last Notice to Mariners and Local Notice to Mariners data that was available when the chart was prepared. Between editions, a chart may be revised; the date of revision will also be shown in the margin.*

the time require for actual printing after the final data input; they are provided to indicate to the user the starting point for keeping the new edition corrected from *Notices*. Most NOS charts are printed to supply a normal demand of one or two years for active areas, and from four to 12 years in areas where few changes occur. (Print-on-Demand charts will carry additional dates indicating the more recent application of information from Notices and other sources.)

Charts may be printed as-is when the stock runs low, but a REVISED PRINT is more likely if a new edition is not published. Revisions include all changes that have been printed in *Notices to Mariners* since the last revision. When major changes occur, such as significant differences between charted depths and actual conditions revealed by new surveys, a NEW EDITION will be published. This will also include all other changes that have been made in aids to navigation, shoreside features, etc.

The NOS is increasingly publishing nautical charts compiled using an automated information system. Every item of information on the chart—every symbol, abbreviation, sounding, line, color, *everything*—is stored on magnetic media as bits of digital data. Negatives for the printing of each color are made by laser beams controlled by a computer. Since a digital database is easily updated, the revision of charts for new editions is becoming an easier and faster process as this technique is extended to all NOS charts. Digitizing also allows downloading of data to electronic charts.

Use only the latest edition of a chart. All new editions supersede older issues, which should be discarded. New editions contain information published in *Notices to Mariners* and *Local Notices to Mariners*. They also include other corrections from extensive application of hydrographic and topographic surveys considered essential for safe navigation but not published in the *Notices*. To ensure that you know what are the latest editions, check the small NOS booklet *Dates of Latest Editions*, issued quarterly and found at local sales agents for charts and other NOS publications; this is also available online at the website www.chartmaker.ncd.noaa.gov and at www.NauticalChart.gov.

Between editions, correct your own charts from information published in *Notices to Mariners* and *Local Notices to Mariners*. Charts kept in stock by the National Ocean Service or sales agents while awaiting sale are not updated or corrected before sale. When you buy a new chart, check all Notices subsequent to the printed edition date and enter all applicable corrections. Changes for NOS charts are also available on the Internet; searches can be made by chart number or by Coast Guard district (but not smaller geographic area). Go to www.chartmaker.ncd.noaa.gov (files may be quite large; a high-speed connection is desirable). Changes for NIMA charts may be derived from *U.S. Notices to Mariners*, available online at http://pollux.nss.nima.mil.

For *Local Notices to Mariners* go to www. navcen.uscg.g ov/lnm.

LATITUDE AND LONGITUDE SCALES

Conventional nautical charts have the geographical north direction toward the top of the sheet, unlike some small-craft charts and chart books that may be oriented to follow the general direction of a river or the coastline without respect to north. Such conventional charts have latitude scales in each side border and longitude scales in the top and bottom borders. Meridians and parallels are drawn across the chart as fine black lines, usually at 2-, 5-, or 10-minute intervals as determined by the scale of the particular chart.

On NOS charts with a scale of 1:50,000 and larger, such as on harbor charts, the subdivisions in the border scales are in terms of minutes and seconds of latitude and longitude; see **Figure I-12**.

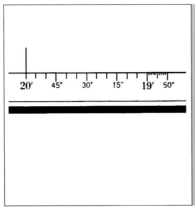

Figure I-12 *On charts at scales of 1:40,000 or larger, latitude and longitude scales are subdivided into minutes and seconds. This extract from a harbor chart shows meridians drawn at 5-minute intervals, tick marks at 1-minute intervals, and a 1-minute interval subdivided into 5-second units. Note the ten 1-second longitude units at the right of the 19′ figure.*

On small-scale charts, the subdivisions are in minutes and fractions of minutes—charts at a scale of 1:80,000, such as *Training Chart 1210TR*, use minutes and tenths of minutes; see **Figure I-13**. Even smaller-scale charts use minutes and fifths or halves, or even full minutes.

Where skewed projections are used, and North is not at the top of the sheet, such as on small-craft charts of the Intracoastal Waterway, divisions of latitude and longitude are indicated along parallels and meridians at several convenient places, and/or separately near the graphic distance scales.

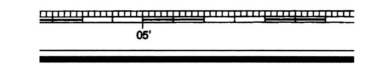

Figure I-13 *On charts of relatively small scale, the latitude and longitude border markings are in minutes and fractions of minutes. On this 1:80,000 chart, meridians are drawn at 10-minute intervals; subdivisions are in minutes and tenths of minutes. On smaller-scale charts, the smallest subdivisions might be fifths, halves, or whole minutes.*

USE OF COLOR ON CHARTS

Nearly all charts use color to emphasize various features and to facilitate reading and interpretation. The colors vary with the agency publishing the chart and its intended use.

The NOS color system uses five multipurpose colors in either solid color or shades—black, magenta, gold, blue, and green. Land areas are a screened tint of gold (urban or built-up areas are often shown in a darker screened tint of that color); water areas are white (the color of the paper), except for the shallower regions, which are shown in a screened blue. Areas that are submerged at some tidal stages but uncovered at others, such as sand bars, mud flats, coral reefs, and marshes, are green. On some charts, water areas that have been swept with wire drags to ensure the absence of isolated rocks or coral heads may be shown by a screened green with the depth of the sweep indicated.

Magenta ink is used for many purposes on charts; it has good visibility under red light, which is used for reading charts during the hours of darkness, because it does not destroy night vision as white light does. Red buoys are printed in magenta, as are red daybeacon symbols. Lighted buoys of any color have a magenta disc over the small circle portion of the symbol to assist in identifying it as a lighted aid. A magenta flare symbol extending from a position dot (much like an exclamation mark) is used with lights, lighted ranges, etc. Caution and danger symbols and notes are printed in magenta; also compass roses, usually, and recommended courses where shown. Black is used for most symbols, contour lines, man-made features, and printed information.

The use of colors on NIMA charts is generally the same as described above for NOS charts, except that gray (screened black) is used for land areas.

LETTERING STYLES

To convey as much information as possible in the clearest form, certain classes of information are printed in one style of lettering and other classes in another style. By knowing what type of lettering is used for which class of information, you can more easily and quickly grasp the data being presented.

Vertical lettering is used for features on NOS charts that are dry at high water and not affected by movement of the water (except for the height of the feature above the water, which may be changed by tidal action). See the use of vertical lettering for the landmark stacks and spires, and the horn signal in **Figure I-14**. Depth information also uses vertical numbers.

Slant (italic) letters, such as those in **Figure I-14**, are used for water, underwater, and floating features, except depth figures. Note also the use in **Figure I-14** of slanted lettering for bottom features and buoy characteristics.

On smaller-scale charts, a small reef (covering and uncovering with tidal action) often cannot be distinguished by symbol from a small islet (always above water); the proper name for either might be "_____ Rock." The feature in doubt is an islet if the name is in vertical letters, but is a reef if lettered in slanting characters. (The small reef would be indicated by a symbol that resembles an asterisk. A small islet would be exaggerated if far enough from shore and filled in with a gold tint.)

Similarly, a piling visible above water at all tidal stages is charted as "Pile," but one beneath the surface is noted as "*Subm pile.*"

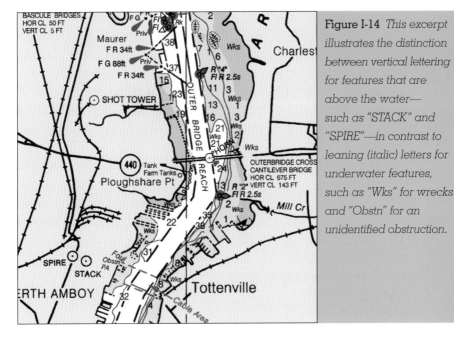

Figure I-14 *This excerpt illustrates the distinction between vertical lettering for features that are above the water— such as "STACK" and "SPIRE"—in contrast to leaning (italic) letters for underwater features, such as "Wks" for wrecks and "Obstn" for an unidentified obstruction.*

Periods after abbreviations are omitted in water and in land areas, but lowercase "i" and "j" are dotted. Periods are used only where needed for clarity, as, for example, in certain notes.

WATER FEATURES

The information shown on charts is a combination of the natural features of the water and land areas and various selected man-made objects and features. Each item shown is carefully chosen for its value to those who navigate vessels of all sizes.

Depths

The principal feature of concern to boaters is DEPTH. For any system of depth information there must be a reference plane, or DATUM. This is obvious in coastal areas, where depths may change hourly as a result of tidal action; it is likewise true in inland areas where lake or river levels may also change, though more slowly on a seasonal basis. Each chart has on it a statement of the datum from which all depths, also called SOUNDINGS, are measured. The choice of the reference plane is based on many factors, most of them technical, but the primary consideration is that of selecting a datum near to normal low-water levels.

Planes of Reference On NOS charts, the datum for the depths is MEAN LOWER LOW WATER; this is of greatest significance in areas such as the Pacific Coast, where each tidal day has two low tides of different heights. However, this datum is now on all NOS charts.

By definition, "mean lower low water" is an average of all lowest water levels for tidal days over a period of time (usually 19 years). Thus, on some days the lower low tide will fall *below* the datum. This will result in *actual* depths being *shallower* than the charted figures. Many charts will have a small box with a tabulation of the extreme variations from charted depths that may be expected for various points; see **Figure I-15**.

Prolonged winds from certain directions, or persistent extremes of barometric pressure, may cause temporary local differences from charted depths. *Remember that there are exceptional conditions at which times the water may be much shallower than indicated on the chart.*

15'

TIDAL INFORMATION

Place		Height referred to datum of soundings (MLLW)			
Name	(LAT/LONG)	Mean Higher High Water	Mean High Water	Mean Low Water	Extreme Low Water
		feet	feet	feet	feet
Plum Gut Harbor (41°10'N/72°12'W)		3.1	2.8	0.2	-3.0
Sag Harbor (41°00'N/72°18'W)		3.0	2.7	0.2	-3.0
Saybrook Jetty (41°16'N/72°21'W)		4.2	3.8	0.3	-3.5
Stratford Shoal (41°04'N/73°06'W)		7.1	6.8	0.2	-3.5

(100)

Figure I-15 *Coast and harbor charts often carry information on the normal range of tides, and the extreme variations from charted depths, that may be expected. Check all newly purchased charts for this important information.*

The datum for water depths in the Great Lakes and other inland bodies of water is an arbitrarily established plane, usually at or near long-term low averages. This datum will be clearly indicated on the chart.

How Depths Are Shown

Depth information is shown on a chart by many small printed figures. These indicate the depth at that point, usually measured in feet or fathoms. Some newer U.S. charts, and many of other nations, measure depth in meters and decimeters (tenths of a meter). The printed depth figures are only a very small fraction of the many soundings taken by the survey team.

Only the more significant and representative depth data are selected for use on the final chart. A skipper can form some opinion of the characteristics of the bottom by noting the density of the depth information. Where depth figures are rather widely spaced, he can be assured of a reasonably flat or uniformly sloping bottom. Wherever the depths vary irregularly or abruptly, the figures will be more frequent and more closely spaced.

Depth Curves Most charts will have contour lines, usually called DEPTH CURVES, connecting points of equal depth. Such lines will appear at certain depths as determined by the scale of the chart, the relative range of depths, and the type of vessel expected to use the chart. Typically, depth curves are shown for 6, 12, 18, 30, and 60 feet, and multiples of 60 feet (note the relationship to fathoms). Depth curves are shown as continuous solid lines with depth labels or various combinations of dots and dashes to code the depth along each line, but it is often easier to learn a line's significance by inspecting of the depth figures on either side of it.

On many charts, a blue tint is shown in water areas out to the curve that is considered to be the danger curve for the majority of important marine traffic that is expected to use that particular chart. In general, the 6-foot curve is considered the danger curve for small-craft and Intracoastal Waterway charts; see **Figure I-16**. The 12- or 18-foot curve is considered the danger curve for harbor charts, and the 30-foot curve for coast and general charts. On some of the latter charts, the area beyond the 18-foot curves may be tinted a lighter shade of blue than the shallower areas. Thus, it can be seen that,

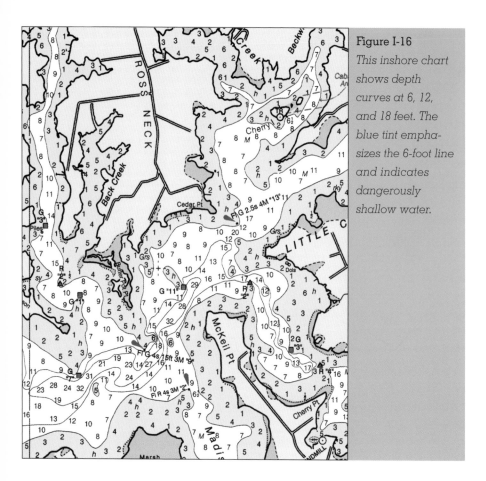

Figure I-16

This inshore chart shows depth curves at 6, 12, and 18 feet. The blue tint emphasizes the 6-foot line and indicates dangerously shallow water.

while blue tint means shallow water, this coloring does not have exactly the same meaning on all charts. Check each chart you plan to use to determine at just what depth the coloring changes.

Isolated offshore areas that have depths corresponding to the tinted areas alongshore waters will also be tinted in the appropriate shade of blue.

Charts without depth curves or dashed curves must be used with caution, as soundings may be too scarce to allow the lines to be drawn accurately.

Avoid an isolated sounding that is shallower than surrounding depths, particularly with a solid or dotted-line ring (depth curve) around it, as it may be doubtful how closely the spot has been examined and whether the least depth has been found.

Dredged Channels

Dredged channels are shown on a chart by two dashed lines to represent the side limits of the improvement. The channel's depth and the date on which such data were obtained are often shown within the lines or close alongside; refer to **Figure I-14**. A dredged basin will be similarly outlined with printed information on depths and date. The depth shown, such as "*6 Feet Oct 2001*," is the controlling depth through the channel on the date shown, but does not mean this depth exists over the full width of the channel; some charts may indicate that the stated depth is only "on centerline."

Channels are sometimes described in terms of specific width as well as depth; for example, "*8 Feet for a Width of 100 Feet*"; a date for this information is often included. Depths may have subsequently changed from either shoaling or further dredging, so if your boat's draft is close to the depth shown for the channel, get local information, if you can, before entering. Detailed information for many dredged channels is shown in tabular form on applicable charts, with revisions of the data published in *Notices to Mariners* or *Local Notices to Mariners* as changes occur.

Nature of the Bottom

For many areas, abbreviations indicate the nature of the bottom, such as sand, rock, mud, grass, or "hard" or "soft." This information is especially valuable when you are anchoring, so take advantage of it wherever it appears. The meanings of these and other abbreviations are usually given on the face of the chart near the basic identification block; many are self-evident.

The Shoreline

The shoreline shown on charts is the MEAN HIGH-WATER LINE for tidal areas; it is the HIGH-WATER LINE in lakes and nontidal areas, except in marsh or mangrove areas, where the outer edge of vegetation is used. Natural shoreline is represented by a slightly heavier line than man-made shoreline. Unsurveyed shoreline, or shoreline connecting two surveys that do not join satisfactorily, is shown by a dashed line. The low-water line is marked by a single row of dots. The outer limits of marsh are indicated by a fine solid line. The region between the high- and low-water lines is tinted green, and may be labeled "Marsh," "Grass," "Mud," "Sand," etc.

FEATURES OF LAND AREAS

Features and characteristics of land areas are shown on nautical charts in only such detail as will assist a navigator on the water. Details are usually confined to those near the shoreline or of such a prominent nature as to be clearly visible for some distance off-shore.

How Topography Is Shown

The general topography of land areas is indicated by CONTOURS, form lines, or hachures. Contours are lines connecting points of equal elevation. Their specific height, usually measured in feet, may be shown by figures placed at suitable points along the lines. The interval of height between adjacent contours is uniform over any one chart. On NOS charts of tidal areas, heights are measured from a different datum than are depths; usually this is Mean High Water; in nontidal areas, the same datum is established for both depths and heights.

FORM LINES, or SKETCH CONTOURS, are shown by broken lines and are contour approximations meant to indicate terrain formations without giving exact information on height. They are used in areas where accurate data are not available to do otherwise. The interval between form lines is not necessarily uniform, and no height figures are given.

HACHURES are short lines or groups of lines that indicate the approximate location of steep slopes. The lines follow the general direction of the slope, with the length of the lines indicating the height of the slope.

Cliffs, Vegetation and The Shore

Cliffs are represented by bands of irregular hachures. The symbol is not an exact "plan view," but rather somewhat of a "side elevation"; its extent is roughly proportional to the height of the cliff. For example, a perpendicular cliff of 100 feet height will be shown by a hachured band wider than one representing a cliff of 15 feet with slope.

Spot elevations are normally given on nautical charts only for summits or the tops of conspicuous landmarks; see **Figure I-17**.

The type of vegetation on land will sometimes be indicated by symbols or wording where this information may be useful to mariners.

The nature of the shore is sometimes indicated by various symbols—rows of fine dots denote a sandy beach, small circles indicate gravel, or irregular shapes mean boulders.

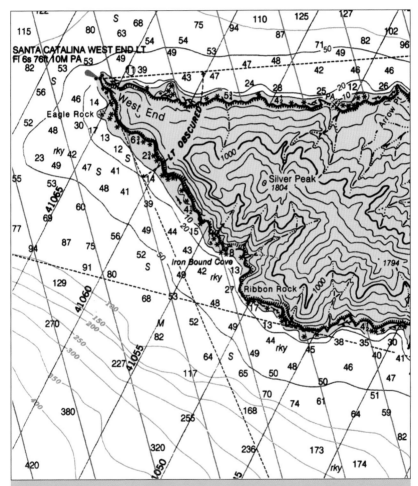

Figure I-17 *Landforms are shown by contour lines and the tops of conspicuous landmarks are identified by height and name. Heights are usually measured from mean high water in feet. The metric system is used on some charts.*

MAN-MADE FEATURES

Man-made features on land are shown in detail to the extent that they can be useful to waterborne traffic. Examples are piers, bridges, overhead power cables, and breakwaters. Other man-made features on land, such as built-up areas, roads, and streets, may be shown in some detail or generalized as determined by their usefulness to navigation and the scale of the chart. On large-scale charts, the actual network of streets may be shown with public buildings such as the post office and customhouse individually identified; see **Figure I-18**, upper. On less detailed charts, the town or city may be represented by a crosshatched or more heavily screened area for the approximate limits of the built-up area, with major streets and road shown by single heavy lines; see **Figure I-18**, lower.

Locations of prominent isolated objects, tanks, stacks, spires, etc., are shown accurately so they may be used for taking bearings.

Specific descriptive names have been given to certain types of landmark objects to standardize terminology. Among the more often used are the following:

- BUILDING or HOUSE—the appropriate term is used when the entire structure is a landmark, rather than any individual feature of it.
- CHIMNEY—a relatively small projection for conveying smoke from a building to the atmosphere. This term is used when the building is more prominent than the chimney but a better bearing can be taken on the smaller feature.
- CUPOLA—a dome-shaped tower or turret rising from a building, generally small in comparison with the building.
- DOME—a large, rounded, hemispherical structure rising above a building; for example, the dome of the United States Capitol in Washington.
- FLAGPOLE—a single staff from which flags are displayed. This term is used when the pole is not attached to a building.
- FLAGSTAFF—a flagpole arising from a building.
- LOOKOUT STATION or Watchtower—a tower surmounted by a small house from which a watch is regularly kept.

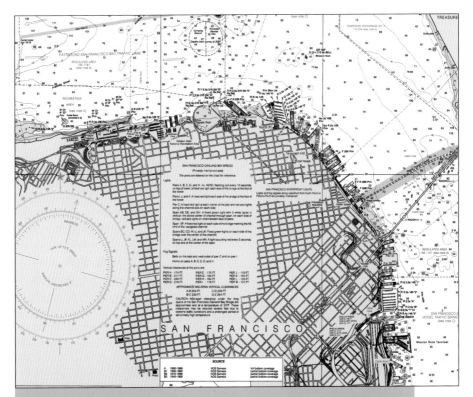

Figure I-18 *On relatively large-scale charts (upper) detailed information may be shown of the streets and buildings of a city or town, particularly near the waterfront. Some street names may be given, as well as the location of public buildings such as a customhouse or post office. On smaller-scale charts (lower) cities, towns, and built-up areas are indicated by cross-hatching, as shown, or by heavier screening that shows up as a darker, but not black, area. Single heavy lines indicate principal roads.*

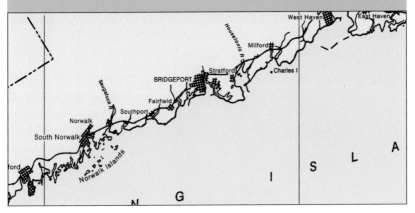

- RADIO MAST—a relatively short pole or slender structure for elevating ratio antennas; usually found in groups.
- RADIO TOWER—a tall pole or structure for elevating ratio antennas.
- SPIRE—a slender, pointed structure extending above a building. It is seldom less than two-thirds of the entire height of the structure, and its lines are rarely broken by intermediate structures. Spires are typically found on churches.
- STACK—a tall smokestack or chimney. This term is used when the stack is more prominent as a landmark than are the accompanying buildings.
- STANDPIPE—a tall cylindrical structure whose height is several times its diameter.
- TANK—a water tank elevated high aboveground by a tall skeleton framework. GAS TANK and OIL TANK are terms used for distinctive structures of specialized design; these structures and are usually lower than a water tank and not supported by a skeleton framework.
- TOWER—any structure with its base on the ground and high in proportion to its base; alternatively, that part of a structure higher than the rest but having essentially vertical sides for the greater part of its height.
- TREE—an isolated, conspicuous tree useful as a navigational landmark (seldom used).

Bridges over navigable waterways are shown with the type of bridge—bascule, swing, suspension, etc.—and both horizontal and vertical clearances in feet, the latter measured from mean *high* water (or other shoreline plane of reference used for heights of objects). Vertical clearance should be stated as the height available at the lowest point over the channel; this "low steel" figure for arched bridges may be supplemented by a sign indicating the amount of additional clearance available at the center. Some bridges will have a sign merely stating "Clearance at Center."

When two similar objects are so located that separate landmark symbols cannot be used, the word "TWIN" is added to the identifying name or abbreviation. When only one of a group of similar objects is charted, a descriptive legend is added in parentheses; for example "(TALLEST OF FOUR)" or "(NORTHEAST OF THREE)."

Radio broadcasting station (AM) antennas are shown on charts where they may be used for taking visual or radio bearings. The call letters and frequency are often shown adjacent to the symbol marking the location of the towers.

Stacks, radio towers, and other tall towers are required to have lights to indicate their presence to aircraft. When these lights are useful for marine navigation, they appear on charts as "FR," "Occ R," or "Fl R"; see page 493. Also there are structures with multiple very-high-intensity, very-short-flash lights that are charted as "Strobe." These are visible in daylight as well as at night and eliminate the need for the tower or stack to be painted with alternating red and white bands.

D

SYMBOLS
AND
ABBREVIATIONS

The vast amount of information shown on a chart, and the closeness of many items, necessitate an extensive use of symbols and abbreviations. You should be familiar with all symbols and abbreviations on the charts you use. You must be able to read and interpret your charts quickly and accurately; the safety of your boat may depend on this ability.

INTERNATIONAL STANDARDS

Chart SYMBOLS are conventional shapes and designs indicating the presence of a certain feature or object at the location shown. No attempt is made at an accurate or detailed representation of the object, but the correct location is shown. Symbols and abbreviations used on NOS and NIMA charts are standardized and appear in a small pamphlet as *Chart No. 1*; see **Figure I-19**. This is also available as a CD-ROM and on the Internet at http://pollux.nss.nima.mil/pubs or at www.chartmaker.ncd.noaa.gov. Generally similar information is printed on the reverse side of *Training Chart 1210TR*. The symbols and abbreviations conform generally with worldwide usage as adopted by the International Hydrographic Organization (IHO).

The standardized symbols and abbreviations are shown in this book on pages 62–152.

CHART NO. 1
UNITED STATES OF AMERICA
NAUTICAL CHART
Symbols Abbreviations and Terms

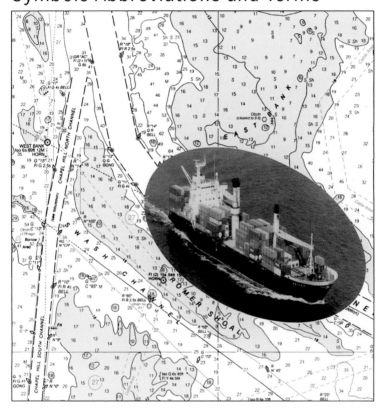

Figure I-19 *Chart No. 1 is not really a "chart" at all. It is a most useful booklet showing all chart symbols used on U.S. charts and the charts of other national jurisdictions.*

BASIC SYMBOLS AND ABBREVIATIONS

Simple inspection of many symbols will reveal a pattern in the way that they are formed. If you know the general principles of chart symbols, you'll have an easier time learning the details.

Buoys

Buoys, except mooring buoys, are shown by a diamond-shaped symbol and a small open circle indicating their position. (A circle is used rather than a position dot in recognition of the fact that a buoy will swing about its anchor on a length of chain.) To avoid interference with other features on the chart, it is often necessary to show the diamond shapes at various angles to the circle; the orientation of the diamond shape has no significance.

On charts using the normal number of colors, RED BUOYS are printed in magenta; the letter "R" may also be shown adjacent to the symbol. GREEN BUOYS are shown in that color with the letter "G" nearby.

A buoy symbol with a line across its *shorter* axis indicates a HORIZONTALLY BANDED BUOY. For a JUNCTION BUOY, both colors are used; magenta (for red) over green, or green over magenta, as the buoy itself is painted. The letters "RG" or "GR," respectively, appear near the symbol.

An open buoy symbol with a line across its *longer* axis represents a VERTICALLY STRIPED BUOY. No colors are used on this symbol; the colors are indicated by the abbreviation "RW" for red-and-white.

Special-purpose buoys are shown by an open, uncolored symbol and the letter "Y."

The type and shape of UNLIGHTED BUOYS are normally indicated by an abbreviation such as "C" for can or "N" for nun.

Because they are a potential hazard to navigation, "superbuoys" are charted with a special symbol; see **Figure I-20**. This category includes exposed location buoys, offshore data collection buoys, and buoys for mooring tankers offshore while loading or unloading.

LIGHTED BUOYS are indicated by a small magenta disc over the small circle that marks the buoy's position. The color and rhythm of the light, and the "hull" colors are indicated by abbreviations near the symbol.

Daybeacons

The symbol for DAYBEACONS—unlighted fixed aids to navigation—may be either a small triangle or a square.

The square symbol, colored green and with the letter "G" nearby, is used for daybeacons that have a solid green dayboard of this shape.

The triangle symbol, colored magenta and with the letter "R" nearby, is used for daybeacons with solid red dayboards of this shape.

The symbol for a daybeacon with red-over-green triangular daymarks is an open triangle with the letters "RG"; for a daybeacon with green-over-red square daymarks, it is an open square symbol with the letters "GR." The symbol for an articulated daybeacon is the usual square or triangle with a small circle added to the bottom, as in **Figure I-20**, labeled "ART."

All octagonal, diamond-shaped, round, or rectangular daymarks will be represented by open square symbols and letter abbreviations as appropriate for the colors concerned.

Figure I-20 *Special chart symbols are used to indicate the position of large automatic navigation buoys, tanker terminal buoys, and ocean data buoys— all types known as "superbuoys."*

Lights, All Types

The chart symbol for lights of all sizes—from the simplest light on a single pile in inland waters to the largest of primary seacoast lights—is the same. This is a black position dot with a magenta "flare" giving much the appearance of a large exclamation mark. In addition to color and characteristics, there may be information on the height of the light and its nominal range (making no allowances for curvature of the earth or observer's height of eye).

The symbol for an articulated light combines the small circle of the buoy symbol and the magenta flare for a fixed light.

Fog Signals

The type of FOG SIGNAL on buoys and lights so equipped is indicated by a descriptive word or abbreviation adjacent to the chart symbol.

Identification by Number

Buoys and lights are usually NUMBERED (or less frequently, designated with letters or combinations of letters and numbers). This identification is placed on the chart near the symbol and is enclosed in quotation marks to distinguish the figures from depth data or other numbers. Primary and some secondary lights are named; the words, abbreviated as necessary, are printed near the symbol where space permits.

Ranges

RANGES are indicated by the two symbols of the front and rear markers (lights or daybeacons), plus a line joining them and extending beyond. This line is solid only over the distance for which the range is to be used for navigation; it continues on as a dashed line to the front marker and on to the rear marker; see **Figure I-21**.

Dangers to Navigation

Symbols are also used for many types of DANGERS to navigation. Differentiation is made between rocks that are awash at times and those which remain below the surface at all tides; between visible wrecks and submerged ones; and between hazards that have been definitely located and those whose position is doubtful. There are a number of symbols and abbreviations for objects and areas dangerous to navigation. Spend adequate time studying them, with emphasis on the types commonly found in your home waters.

Accuracy and Precision Problems

The art and science of navigation has not been immune from the advances of technology. The most obvious new technology in piloting is the Differential Global Positioning System (DGPS). Navigation systems using DGPS for locating a vessel's position have put mariners in a counterintuitive predicament. In many cases, the DGPS position is more accurate than the technology that was used to put the soundings and features on the chart.

This discrepancy is even more pronounced when the chart scale is taken into consideration. The width of a line or line symbol on a paper chart is typically 0.1 to 1.5 millimeters (0.004 to 0.06 inches). A feature's actual position can fall anywhere within that line or symbol. Thus, on a typical 1:40,000 harbor chart, a feature could have a potential error of 40 to 80 meters (130 to 260 feet) due to scale alone; a line plotted on a chart would have a similar range of possible error.

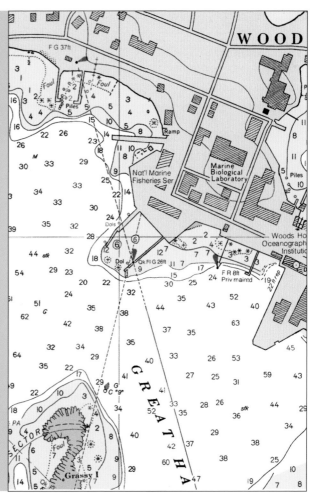

Figure I-21 *Ranges are excellent aids to navigation; they are charted by showing the front and rear marks (lighted or unlighted) with a line between them that denotes the range. The line is solid over the portion that is to be navigated, and dashed where it should not be followed.*

DGPS errors do not normally exceed a few meters (10 to 15 feet), and are often less. This is often the cause of the "ship on pier situation" in which a vessel made fast to a pier shows on an electronic navigation system as being on the pier rather than alongside it.

THE CHART NUMBERING SYSTEM

Numbering in NOS and NIMA charts shares a common system. This is based on REGIONS and SUBREGIONS. Boaters will generally be concerned only with charts having *five-digit* numbers; such charts have a scale of 1:2,000,000 or larger. The first digit refers to a region of the world, and the second, together with the first, to a subregion; the final three digits are assigned systematically within the subregion to denote the specific chart.

Region 1 includes the waters in and around the United States and Canada. Region 2 covers Central and South America, Mexico, the Bahamas, and the West Indies.

Region 1 has nine subregions designated counterclockwise around North America, from Subregion 11 for the Gulf of Mexico and the Atlantic Coast up to Cape Hatteras. Subregion 12 extends to the eastern tip of Long Island, and 13 extends to the Canadian border. Subregion 14 covers the Great Lakes; Subregion 18 is the U.S. Pacific Coast; Subregion 19 covers the Hawaiian Islands and adjacent waters. **Figure I-22** shows the regions and subregions of the world.

The final three digits of a five-digit number are assigned counterclockwise around the subregion or along the coast. Many numbers are skipped over and left unassigned so that future charts can be fitted into the system.

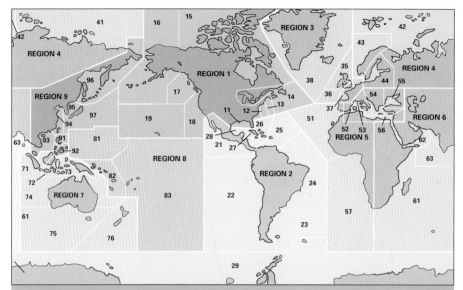

Figure I-22 *This diagram shows the chart regions and subregions of the world. Region 1 covers the United States and Canada. The number of the subregion forms the first two digits of a five-digit chart number.*

THE FIVE NOS CHART SERIES

As previously mentioned, charts are published in a wide range of scales. For general convenience of reference, the NOS has classified charts into "series," as follows:

• SAILING CHARTS—the smallest scale charts covering long stretches of coastline; for example, Cape Sable, Newfoundland, to Cape Hatteras, North Carolina; the Gulf of Mexico; or San Francisco to Cape Flattery, Washington; see **Figure I-23**. The charts in this series are published at scales of 1:600,000 or smaller. Sailing charts are prepared for the use of the navigator in fixing his position as he approaches the coast from open ocean, or when sailing between distant coastal ports. They show the offshore soundings, the principal lights and outer buoys, and landmarks visible at great distances. Other than for ocean cruising races, the average boater will have little use for charts in this series, except perhaps to plot the paths of hurricanes and other tropical disturbances.

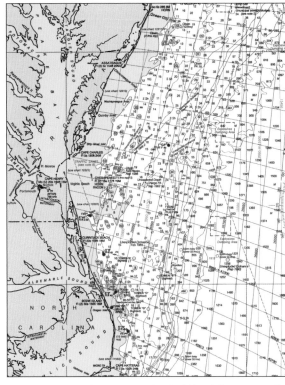

Figure I-23 *Sailing chart 13003, Cape Sable, Nova Scotia, to Cape Hatteras, North Carolina, scale 1:1,200,000. This chart would be used for far off-shore passages; it shows very little detail of inshore aids to navigation. The entrance to Chesapeake Bay is just above the middle of this chart extract. On this chart, 1 inch equals 16.46 nautical miles.*

• GENERAL CHARTS—The second series comprises charts with scales in the range of 1:150,000 to 1:600,000. These cover more limited areas, such as Cape May, New Jersey to Cape Hatteras, North Carolina, Mississippi River to Galveston Bay; or San Francisco to Point Arena, California. General charts are intended for coastwise navigation outside of offshore reefs and shoals when the vessel's course is mostly within sight of land and her position can be fixed by landmarks, lights, buoys, and soundings; see **Figure I-24**.

• COAST CHARTS—This next-larger scale series consists of charts for close-in coastwise navigation, for entering and leaving harbors, and for navigating large inland bodies of water. The scales used range from 1:50,000 to 1:150,000, with most being 1:80,000; see **Figure I-25.** Typical examples of coast charts are the widely used *Training Chart No. 1210TR,* and such navigational charts as the series of five which covers Chesapeake Bay, or 18746, which takes the California skipper from Long Beach or Newport to Santa Catalina Island and back. The average boater may use several charts from this series.

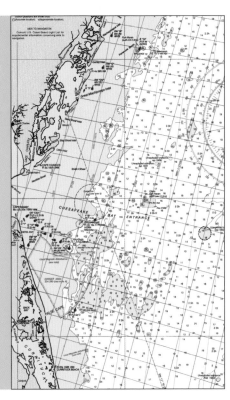

Figure I-24 *General Chart 12200, Cape May to Cape Hatteras, scale 1:419,706. This chart does not extend as far off-shore, and would be used for the initial approach from sea toward Chesapeake Bay Entrance; additional details of aids to navigation are shown. On this chart, 1 inch equals 5.76 nautical miles.*

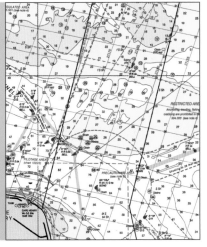

Figure I-25 *Coast Chart 12221, Chesapeake Bay Entrance, scale 1:80,000. This chart gives details of the water depths, hazards, aids to navigation, etc., within the coastline. Its scale of 1 inch to 1.10 nautical miles would be suitable for navigating into the bay.*

• HARBOR CHARTS—This is the largest-scale and most detailed series; see **Figure I-26**. Scales range from 1:50,000 to 1:5,000, with an occasional inset of even larger scale. The scale used

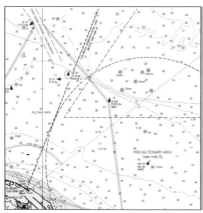

Figure I-26 *Harbor Chart 12222, Cape Charles to Norfolk Harbor, Scale 1:40,000. This chart shows all details of the water and aids to navigation. It can be used for piloting down channels and to anchorages. On this chart, 1 inch equals 0.55 nautical miles.*

for any specific chart is determined by the need for showing detail and by the area to be covered by a single sheet.

• SMALL-CRAFT CHARTS—These compact charts provide the small-craft skipper with a convenient, folded-format chart designed primarily for use in confined spaces; see **Figure I-27**. One of the formats is designed to cover long, narrow waterways; another is a folded multipage chart covering larger areas. All small-craft charts include a tabulation of public marine facilities, tide tables, weather information sources, and similar data of particular value to boaters. This small-craft series is described in greater detail on page 54.

NAUTICAL CHART 12364

NEW HAVEN HARBOR ENTRANCE AND PORT JEFFERSON TO THROGS NECK
LONG ISLAND SOUND
CONNECTICUT - NEW YORK

FIGHT POLLUTION!
KEEP YOUR WATERWAYS CLEAN!

Figure I-27 *For use on small boats, particularly open boats, a small-craft (sc) chart has many advantages over a large, sheet-like, conventional chart. The SC chart can be easily opened only to the area of immediate interest. Additional information, such as facility data and tidal predictions, is also available for the use of boaters.*

Stowage and Use

NOS charts in the first four series listed above are printed by accurate techniques on highly durable paper. Individual charts range in size from about 19 x 26 to 36 x 54 inches. (483 x 660 to 914 x 1,372 mm). Some U.S. charts are now printed in the international standard size of 841 x 1,189 mm (33.1 x 46.8 inches). They are among the navigator's most important tools and should be given careful handling and proper stowage. If circumstances permit, they should be stowed flat or rolled, and in a dry place. Charts of this type should not be folded if this can be avoided.

Make any permanent corrections in ink so they will not be inadvertently erased; make all other lines and notations lightly in pencil so they may be erased without damaging the chart.

SELECTING THE PROPER CHART

From a consideration of the five categories of charts discussed above, you can see that most boating areas will appear on two charts of different series, and that some areas will be covered by three or four charts of different scales. Such charts will vary widely in the extent of the area covered and the amount of detail shown. Choosing the proper chart for your use is important. In general, the closer you are to shoal waters and dangers to navigation, the larger you will want the scale of your chart.

What Coast Charts Show

Coast charts show the major hazards and aids to navigation, and give general information on depths. Some charts in this series entirely omit any details in certain areas that are covered by larger-scale charts. For example, Narragansett Bay appears on Chart 13218, but no details at all are given, merely a small note "(Chart 13221)." Other coast charts include in their area coverage portions of the Atlantic Intracoastal Waterway, but the navigator is referred to the ICW route charts for all information on the inland route. Many coast charts include a small diagram outlining the areas covered by each larger-scale chart. On Chart 13218, this amounts to all portions of 13 more-detailed charts.

What Harbor Charts Show

Harbor charts show more numerous soundings and *all* aids to navigation, and permit the most accurate fixing of position from plotted bearings. The question may be asked, why ever select any but the largest-scale chart? The answer lies in the fact that as the scale is increased, the area covered is proportionately decreased. Thus, for a given cruise, many more charts from the harbor series would be required than from the coast series. Further, in some areas, continuous coverage from port to port is not possible with harbor charts alone. Yet another problem is that the increased number of harbor charts would complicate the task of laying out a long run between ports.

Selecting the proper charts will usually mean that you have a mixture of coast charts for the longer runs and harbor charts for entering ports and exploring up rivers and creeks. For some areas, you will find it useful to have one or more general charts in addition to the coast and harbor charts. For example, the best overall route up Chesapeake Bay is more easily plotted on one general chart, 12280, than on a series of five coast charts, 12221 to 12273. The coast charts will be desirable for the actual trip, however, when used with some harbor charts.

In the margin of many charts, you will find helpful information regarding the next chart to use when you are going in a particular direction. This note will take the form of a statement such as "(Joins Chart 13233)" or "(Continued on Chart 13236)."

SMALL-CRAFT CHARTS

The charts in the first four series discussed on pages 49–52 are referred to as "conventional charts" and are intended for flat or rolled storage. The fifth series, small-craft charts, is quite different, designed for more convenient use in the limited space available on boats, and for folded storage; refer to **Figure I-27**. There are approximately 90 small-craft charts, each numbered in the normal five-digit style.

Types of Small-Craft Charts

Small-craft charts are printed in three general formats termed ROUTE, FOLIO, and AREA, as follows:

• Small-craft ROUTE CHARTS, consisting of a single sheet printed front and back and accordion folded; some are slipped into a suitable jacket. These are sometimes referred to as POCKET FOLD CHARTS.

• Small-craft FOLIO CHARTS, consisting of three or four sheets printed front and back, accordion folded, and bound in a suitable cover.

• Small-craft AREA CHARTS, usually consisting of a conventional chart printed on lightweight paper with additional data for the small-boat skipper. Half the chart is printed on each side of the paper with a slight area of overlap. The chart is accordion folded and may be issued in a protective jacket.

Route and area charts are being redesigned into a 5-inch by 10-inch "pocket fold" format without a cover jacket. All information once shown on the separate jackets is now included in the margins of the chart itself. The elimination of the jacket allows for a lower price.

Facilities Data

A unique feature of these small-craft charts is the variety of data printed on the chart or the protective jacket; see **Figure I-28**. Repair yard and marina locations are clearly marked, and the available services and supplies are tabulated. A tide table for the year, marine weather information, Rules of the Road, whistle signals, and warning notes are included for ready reference.

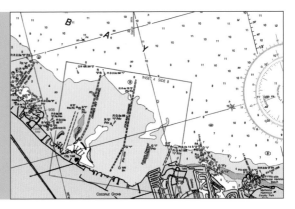

Figure I-28 *Table on a small-craft chart lists the tide ranges, depths, and the services and supplies available at marine facilities in the area covered. The numbers at the left are keyed to locations on the chart.*

Small-craft charts make frequent use of insets to show such features as small creeks and harbors in greater detail at a larger scale.

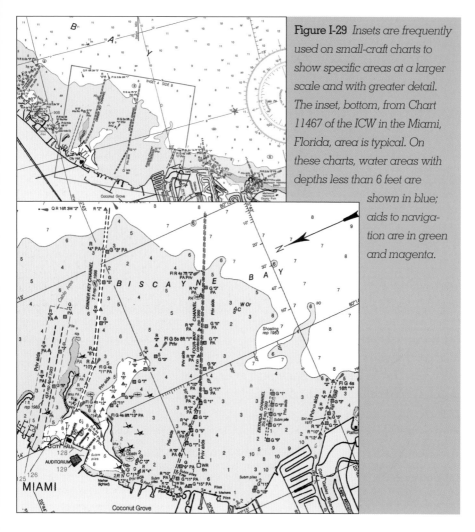

Figure I-29 *Insets are frequently used on small-craft charts to show specific areas at a larger scale and with greater detail. The inset, bottom, from Chart 11467 of the ICW in the Miami, Florida, area is typical. On these charts, water areas with depths less than 6 feet are shown in blue; aids to navigation are in green and magenta.*

Figure I-29 shows an inset from Chart 11467 detailing waters just south of Miami, Florida.

Courses Indicated

Many of the folio and route types of small-craft charts indicate a recommended track to be followed. The longer stretches of these tracks are marked as to *true* course and distance in miles and tenths. Route charts of the Intracoastal Waterway also have numbered marks every five *statute* miles, indicating the accumulated distance southward from Norfolk, Virginia, to Florida, and eastward and westward from Harvey Lock, Louisiana (also westward across the Okeechobee Waterway and northward along the Florida Gulf Coast); see **Figure I-30**. Facilities along the ICW are designated in accordance with a numbering system that starts over again with "1" on each chart of the series.

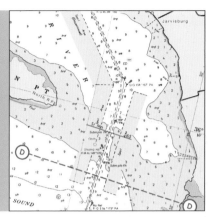

Figure I-30 *Charts of the Atlantic Intracoastal Waterway show a fine magenta line that indicates the route to be followed. Tick marks are placed at five-mile intervals along this course line and are labeled with the accumulated mileage (statute) south from Norfolk, Virginia. The "D—D" line on this excerpt is a matching line to facilitate shifting to the adjoining Intracoastal Waterway chart.*

Periodic Revision

Many, but not all, small-craft charts are revised and reissued annually or biannually, sometimes to coincide with the start of the boating season in the locality concerned. These charts are not hand-corrected by the NOS after they are printed and placed in stock. Check the publication *Dates of Latest Editions* to be sure that you are using the most recent chart, and keep your chart up-to-date between editions by applying all critical changes published in *Notices to Mariners* and *Local Notices to Mariners*. This is not a great chore, *if* you keep up with the changes and don't fall behind.

Other Charts for Small Craft

MODIFIED ROUTE CHARTS are identical in construction and format to small-craft area charts, and are used in areas that are not adaptable to the route chart style used for long, narrow waterways.

RECREATIONAL CHARTS are a series of large-scale charts, published in book format, providing sequential coverage for selected areas.

MARINE FACILITIES CHARTS are conventional charts with small-craft facility information overprinted on the chart and tabulated on the reverse side.

CANOE CHARTS covering the Minnesota–Ontario Border Lakes are designed to meet the needs of operators of small, shallow-draft craft.

GREAT LAKE CHARTS

Polyconic projection is used for most of the NOS charts of the Great Lakes; a few smaller-scale charts are also published in Mercator projection editions, as are all those published in metric editions. Other small variations between these and coastal charts may be noted. Often courses and distances (in statute miles) will be shown for runs between important points.

On the Great Lakes and connecting waters, special editions of charts for small craft are available for a number of boating areas. These are bound into SMALL-CRAFT BOOK CHARTS booklets with individual charts at various scales.

NIMA CHARTS

Charts from the National Imagery and Mapping Agency are used by skippers making long ocean voyages or visiting waters of other nations (except Canada). The way of showing information does not differ much from the more familiar NOS charts; symbols and abbreviations will be familiar to the coastal boater, but land areas are shaded gray rather than gold. Symbols are different for lighted buoys and those with radar reflectors. Most charts based on non–U.S. sources will show depths and heights in meters and fractions, rather than in feet or fathoms; increasingly, NIMA-originated charts will also use metric units.

The NIMA—and it predecessor agency, the Defense Mapping Abency Hydrographic Topograpic Center, or DMAHTC—have published special editions for some of the major ocean sailing races. These are regular editions of the applicable charts, overprinted with additional information for the yachtsman, including the direct rhumb line, typical sailing tracks for seasonal winds, additional current data, and other useful items. These charts are listed in the section on Miscellaneous Charts and Publications in the NIMA *Chart Catalog*.

Remember that many NIMA charts are based on surveys done by other nations; see **Figure I-31**. The authority for the charted information is always given, as is the date of the surveys.

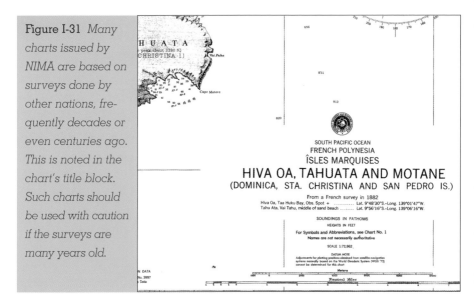

Figure I-31 *Many charts issued by NIMA are based on surveys done by other nations, frequently decades or even centuries ago. This is noted in the chart's title block. Such charts should be used with caution if the surveys are many years old.*

SOUTH PACIFIC OCEAN
FRENCH POLYNESIA
ÎSLES MARQUISES

HIVA OA, TAHUATA AND MOTANE
(DOMINICA, STA. CHRISTINA AND SAN PEDRO IS.)

From a French survey in 1882
Hiva Oa, Taa Huku Bay, Obs. Spot + ... Lat. 9°48'30"S.–Long. 139°01'47"W.
Tahu Ata, Vai Tahu, middle of sand beach .... Lat. 9°56'16"S.–Long. 139°06'16"W.

SOUNDINGS IN FATHOMS
HEIGHTS IN FEET

For Symbols and Abbreviations, see Chart No. 1
Names are not necessarily authoritative

SCALE 1:72,962.

DATUM NOTE
Adjustments for plotting positions obtained from satellite navigation
systems normally based on the World Geodetic System (WGS '72)
cannot be determined for this chart

Meters

Nautical Miles

INLAND RIVER CHARTS

Boaters on inland rivers use charts that differ in many respects from those used in coastal waters. Often the inland river charts are issued in book form with several pages covering successive stretches of a river; frequently, they are called "navigational maps."

Probably the most obvious difference is the usual lack of depth figures. In lieu of these, there is generally a broken line designating the route to be followed. To make the best use of each paper sheet, pages may be oriented differently; North is seldom toward the top, and its actual direction is shown by an arrow. Some symbols may vary slightly in appearance from those on "salt water" charts, and additional ones may be used as required by local conditions. Distances are stated in terms of statute miles, and locations are described in distances *upriver* from a specified origin point.

BATHYMETRIC CHARTS

BATHYMETRIC CHARTS are designed to give maximum emphasis to the configuration of the bottom show depths beyond the 100-fathom curve. They employ depth contours similar to contours shown on land areas to indicate graduations in height.

CAUTIONS REGARDING USE OF CHARTS

Producing charts for the vast coastline and contiguous waterways of the United States is a major undertaking. The U.S. Atlantic coastline exceeds 24,500 nautical miles, the Gulf Coast 15,000 miles, the Pacific Coast 7,000 miles, and the Alaskan and Hawaiian shorelines more than 30,000 nautical miles. The NOS publishes almost 1,000 charts covering more than 3.6 million square miles, and both of these figures increase each year. In meeting its global responsibilities, NIMA puts out charts numbered in the thousands, and there are, in addition, many U.S. Army Corps of Engineers charts and navigational maps.

Keeping so many charts up-to-date is obviously a staggering task. Surveys are constantly being made in new areas and must be rechecked in old areas, but this work generally depends on the limitations of funding by taxpayers through the U.S. Congress. The NOS has an extensive program of cooperative reporting by boaters to supplement its own information-gathering capability. Formal programs are established in the United States Power Squadrons and the U.S. Coast Guard Auxiliary, but *all* individual skippers are encouraged to report any corrections, additions, or comments to the chart's issuing agency. Comments are also desired on other publications such as the *Coast Pilots.* Send comments to the Director, National Ocean Service, Silver Spring, MD 20910-3233.

Charting agencies make every effort to keep their products accurate and up-to-date with changing editions. Major disturbances of nature such as hurricanes along the Atlantic Coast and earthquakes in the Pacific Northwest cause sudden and extensive changes in hydrography, and destroy aids to navigation. The everyday forces of wind and waves cause slower and less obvious changes in channels and shoals.

Be alert to the possibility of changes. Most charts will cite the authorities for the information presented and frequently the date of the information. Use additional caution when the surveys date back many years. Half of NOS charts are based on surveys made before 1940, many using lead lines. The surveys of some NIMA charts go back more than a century.

Another possible problem lies in the HORIZONTAL DATUM used on the chart. Various datums have been used over the years; the standard now is the 1984 World Geodetic System (WGS 84). The 1983 North American Datum is essentially the same, but other datums may be found on charts from other regions or nations that will require adjustments to positions of charted features. This is primarily of concern to vessels using electronic navigation systems.

Chart No. 1

A Chart Number, Title, Marginal Notes

Schematic layout of an NOS chart (reduced in size)

DEPTHS IN METERS   Nautical Chart Catalog No3 Panel I, M

54°56'00" N

⑨ 08°36'00" W

INTERNATIONAL

⑫

CHART SERIES

UNITED STATES

ALASKA – SOUTH COAST

⑩ **COOK INLET**

Mercator Projection
⑬ Scale 1:100,000 at Lat 54°00'

Authorities

⑪

Note A

Pipelines

⑯

Caution

104

104

⑮

⑰

(JOINS CHART INT 513)

Submarine Operating
Area 207.640
(see note A)

⑯

53°54'00"N

⑨ 08°32'00" W

Inset

⑮

Source

⑦

Unimak Pass
1:12500
⑭

53°51'00"N

08°21'00" W

⑨

08°06'00" W

53°06'00"N

⑧

(740,9 × 1103,9 mm)

Chart Number, Title, Marginal Notes

*Magnetic Features → **B***	*Tidal Data → **H***
	*Decca, Loran-C, Omega → **S***

①	Chart number in national chart series
②	Identification of a latticed chart (if any): D for Decca LC for Loran-C Om for Omega
③	Chart number in international chart series (if any)
④	Publication note (imprint)
⑤	Bar Code and Stock Numbers
⑥	Edition note: In the example: Seventh edition published in June, 1996
⑦	Source data diagram (if any). For attention to navigators: use caution where surveys are inadequate.
⑧	Dimensions of inner borders
⑨	Corner co-ordinates
⑩	Chart title } May be quoted when ordering a chart, in addition to chart number
⑪	Explanatory notes on chart construction, etc. To be read before using chart
⑫	Seals: In the example, the national and international Hydrographic Organization seals show that this national chart is also an international one. Purely national charts have the national seal only. Reproductions of charts of other nations (facsimile) have the seals of the original producer (left), publisher (center) and the IHO (right).
⑬	Projection and scale of chart at stated latitude. The scale is precisely as stated only at the latitude quoted
⑭	Linear scale on large-scale charts
⑮	Reference to a larger-scale chart
⑯	Cautionary notes (if any). Information on particular features, to be read before using chart
⑰	Reference to an adjoining chart of similar scale

B *Positions, Distances, Directions, Compass*

Geographical Positions

1	Lat	Latitude	Lat
2	Long	Longitude	Long
3		International meridian (Greenwich)	
4	°	Degree(s)	°
5	′	Minute(s) of arc	′
6	″	Second(s) of arc	″
7	PA	Position approximate	PA
8	PD	Position doubtful	PD
9	N	North, Northern	N
10	E	East, Eastern	E
11	S	South, Southern	S
12	W	West, Western	W
13	NE	Northeast	NE
14	SE	Southeast	SE
15	NW	Northwest	NW
16	SW	Southwest	SW

Control Points

20	△	Triangulation point	△
21	⊕ Obs Spot	Observation spot	⊕
22	⊙	Fixed point	⊚
23	○ BM	Benchmark	⊤
24	◇ Bdy Mon	Boundary mark	

Symbolized Positions (Examples)

30		⌗ 🔟 Wk (PA)	Symbols in plan: position is center of primary symbol	ⵘ ⌗ 🔟 Wk (PA)
31		⚓ ⸙	Symbols in profile: position is at bottom of symbol	⚓ ⚓ ⸙ ⸙
32	⊙	Point symbols (accurate positions)	⊙ Mast ⊙ MAST
33	○	Approximate position	○ Mast PA

Positions, Distances, Directions, Compass

Units

	km	Kilometer(s)	km	
	m	Meter(s)	m	
	dm	Decimeter(s)	dm	
	cm	Centimeter(s)	cm	
	mm	Millimeter(s)	mm	
	M, Mi, NMi, NM	Nautical (mile(s) (1852m) or sea mile(s)	M	
	cbl	Cable(s) length		
	ft	Foot/feet	ft	
	fm, fms	Fathom(s)		
	h, hr	Hour	h	
	m, min	Minute(s) of time	m	min
	s, sec	Second(s) of time	s	sec
	kn	Knot(s)	kn	
	t	Ton(s) (metric ton equals 2,204.6 lbs)	t	
	cd	Candela (new candle)	cd	

Magnetic Compass

	var VAR	Variation	
	mag	magnetic	
	brg	Bearing	
	T	true	
		decreasing	
		increasing	
		Annual change	
	dev	Deviation	
1		Note of magnetic variation, in position	Magnetic Variation 4°31'W 1995 (8'E)
2		Note of magnetic variation, out of position	Magnetic Variation at 55°N 8°W 4°31'W 1995 (8'E)

| 70 | Compass rose, normal pattern (smaller patterns of compass rose may be used) |

Magnetic Variation (example): 4°15′ W 1997 (8′ E) *on magnetic north arrow means Magnetic Variation 4°15′ W in 1997, annual change 8′E (i.e. magnetic variation decreasing 8′ annually).*

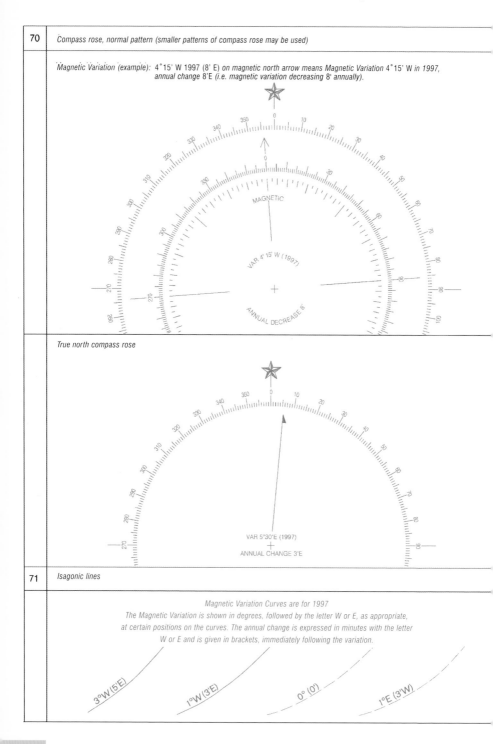

True north compass rose

| 71 | Isagonic lines |

Magnetic Variation Curves are for 1997
The Magnetic Variation is shown in degrees, followed by the letter W or E, as appropriate,
at certain positions on the curves. The annual change is expressed in minutes with the letter
W or E and is given in brackets, immediately following the variation.

Positions, Distances, Directions, Compass

.1	+15°	Local magnetic disturbances *Within the enclosed area the magnetic variation may deviate from the normal by the value shown.*	±15°
.2	**Local Magnetic Disturbance** (see Note)	*Where the area affected cannot be easily defined, a legend only is shown at the position.*	**Local Magnetic Anomaly** (see Note)

Supplementary National Symbols

m²	*Square meter*	
m³	*Cubic meter*	
in, ins	*inch(es)*	
yd, yds	*Yard(s)*	
St M, St Mi	*Statute mile*	
μsec, μs	*Microsecond*	
Hz	*Hertz*	
kHz	*Kilohertz*	
MHz	*Megahertz*	
cps, c/s	*Cycles/second*	
kc	*Kilocycle*	
Mc	*Megacycle*	
T	*Ton (U.S. short ton equals 2,000 lbs)*	
deg	*Degree(s)*	

C *Natural Features*

Coastline			Supplementary national symbols: a – e

Foreshore → I, J

1		Coastline, surveyed	
2		Coastline, unsurveyed	
3	high low	Steep coast, Steep coast with rock cliffs, Cliffs	
4		Coastal hillocks, elevation not determined	
5		Flat coast	
6		Sandy shore	
7		Stony shore, Shingly shore	Stone
8		Sandhills, Dunes	Dunes
9	Marsh	Apparent Shoreline	
9.1		Vegetation or topographic Feature Area Limit in general	

68 CHART NO. 1

Natural Features

Supplementary national symbols: f, g

lane of Reference for Heights → H

	Contour lines with spot height	
· 256	Spot heights	
	Approximate contour lines with approximate height	
	Form lines with spot height	
	Approximate height of top of trees (above height datum)	

ater Features, Lava

Supplementary national symbols: h

	River, Stream	
	Intermittent river	
	Rapids, Waterfalls	
	Lakes	

C *Natural Features*

24		Salt pans	S a l t p a
25		Glacier	
26		Lava flow	

Vegetation			*Supplementary national symbols:* **i** -
30	Wooded	Wood, in general	W o o d e
31		Prominent trees (in groups or isolated)	
31.1		Deciduous tree	
31.2		Evergreen (except conifer)	
31.3		Conifer	
31.4		Palm	
31.5		Nipa palm	
31.6		Casuarina	
31.7		Filao	
31.8		Eucalyptus	

Natural Features

Mangrove / (used in small areas)	Mangrove		
Marsh (used in small areas)	Marsh		M a r s h
Swamp	Swamp		
Cypress	Cypress		

Uncovers	Chart sounding datum line (surveyed)	
	Approximate sounding datum line (inadequately surveyed)	
Mud	Foreshore; Strand (in general) Stones; Shingle; Gravel; Mud; Sand	
Breakers Breakers (if extensive)	Breakers along a shore	

C *Natural Features*

e		Rubble	
f	610 606	Hachures	
g		Shading	
h		Lagoon	
i	Wooded	Deciduous woodland	
j	Wooded	Coniferous woodland	
k		Tree plantation	
l	Cultivated	Cultivated fields	
m	Grass	Grass fields	
n	Rice	Paddy (rice) fields	
o	Bushes	Bushes	

Cultural Features

Settlements, Buildings

Height of objects → E				Landmarks → E	
		Urban area			
		Settlement with scattered buildings			
⌐	#	o	Settlement (on medium and small-scale charts)l	o Name	▭ Name
Vil			Village	✠ Name	■ Name HOTEL
■	▨	▢	Buildings in general	▪ ▪ ▭ ▭	
▨▨▨	▭		Important building in built-up area	Hotel	Hotel
Church Street			Street name, Road name	St Street Ave Avenue Blvd Boulevard	N A M E
▭ Ruins	o Ru		Ruins, Ruined landmark	Ru	⛉ Ru

Roads, Railways, Airfields

Supplementary national symbols: a-c

══════	Motorway	
═ ═ ═ ═ ═	Road (hard surfaced)	═══ ═══
- - - - - - - - -	Track, Path (lose or unsurfaced)	- - - - - - = = = = =
┼──■──┼	Railway, with station	
▦▦▦▦▦▦▦▦	Cutting	

D Cultural Features

15		Embankment	
16		Tunnel	
17		Airport, Airfield	Air-field

Other Cultural Features

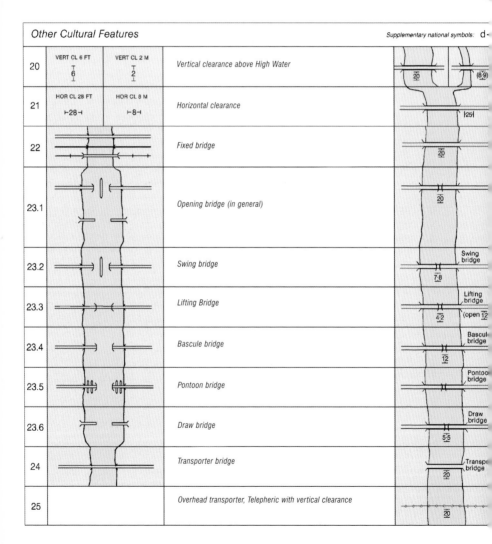

20	VERT CL 6 FT 6	VERT CL 2 M 2	Vertical clearance above High Water	20 (8'9)
21	HOR CL 28 FT ⊢28⊣	HOR CL 8 M ⊢8⊣	Horizontal clearance	¦25¦
22			Fixed bridge	20
23.1			Opening bridge (in general)	20
23.2			Swing bridge	Swing bridge 7·8
23.3			Lifting Bridge	Lifting bridge 4·2 (open 12
23.4			Bascule bridge	Bascul bridge 12
23.5			Pontoon bridge	Pontoo bridge
23.6			Draw bridge	Draw bridge 5·5
24			Transporter bridge	Transp bridge 20
25			Overhead transporter, Telepheric with vertical clearance	20

Cultural Features

OVERHEAD POWER CABLE AUTHORIZED CL 140 FT / TOWER / TOWER	Power transmission line with pylons and safe overhead clearance	Pyl — s —⊙— ◆— s — Pyl —⊙— ◆— s / s 20 s
Tel	Overhead cable, Telephone line, Telegraph line	—————●—————— / 20
OVHD PIPE VERT CL 6 FT	Overhead pipe with vertical clearance	Overhead pipe / 20
	Pipeline on land	

Supplementary National Symbols

20 50 95	Highway markers	
CONRAIL / Same grade / Ry above / Ry below	Railway (Ry) (single or double track) Railroad (RR)	
	Abandoned railroad	
	Bridge under construction	
	Footbridge	
Viaduct	Viaduct	
●———————————●	Fence	
	Power transmission line	

E *Landmarks*

Plane of reference for Heights → H   Lighthouses → P   Beacons → Q

General

1	⊙TANK o Tk ⊕ ⊘		Examples of landmarks	◆ Building ⊙ Hotel
2	⊙ CAPITOL DOME ⊙ WORLD TRADE CENTER		Examples of conspicuous landmarks	◆ FACTORY WATER TR ⊙ HOTEL WATER TOWER
3.1			Pictorial symbols (in true position)	
3.2			Sketches, Views (out of position)	
4		(30)	Height of top of a structure above plane of reference for heights	(30)
5		(̄30̄)	Height of structure above ground level	(̄30̄)

Landmarks

10.1	✝ Ch		Church	⊹	Ch	⊹
10.2			Church tower	⊹ Tr	Tr	
10.3	⊙SPIRE o Spire		Church spire	⊹ Sp	Sp	
10.4	⊙CUPOLA o Cup		Church cupola	⊹ Cup	Cup	♀
11	✚ Ch		Chapel			‡
12	⚇		Cross, Calvary			+ ±
13	⊠		Temple	⊠		⊕
14	⊠		Pagoda	⊠		
15	⊠		Shinto shrine, Josshouse	⊠		卐

Landmarks

	⌧	Buddhist temple	⌧ 卍	
	⌷ ⏧ ⌗	Mosque, Minaret	⌷	⌗ ⌷
	⊡ ⏧	Marabout	⊙ Marabout	
Cem	⊞ Cem	Cemetery (for all religious demoninations)	L L L L L L L L L L L L	u u u
⊙ TOWER o Tr		Tower	⍠ Tr	
⊙ STANDPIPE ⊙ WTR TR o S'pipe o Wtr Tr		Standpipe Water tower, Water tank on a tower	⍟	
⊙ CHIMNEY o Chy		Chimney	⍟ ⌾ Chy	⍟
⊙ FLARE o Flare		Flare stack (on land)	⍟	
MONUMENT ⊙ o Mon		Monument	⍟ Mon	⍟ ⊙
⊙WINDMILL ⊙WINDMILL o Windmill ⊗		Windmill	⤫	⍟ ⤫
		Windmill (wingless)	⤫ Ru	
⊙ WINDMOTOR o Windmotor		Windmotor	⍟	⤫ ⤫
⊙ F S ⊙ F P o F S o F P		Flagstaff, Flagpole	� FS	
⊙ R MAST ⊙ TV MAST o R Mast o TV Mast		Radio mast, Television mast	⍟	
⊙ R TR ⊙ TV TR o R Tr o TV Tr		Radio tower, Television tower	⍟	
⊙ RADAR MAST o Radar Mast		Radar mast	⊙ Radar Mast	

E Landmarks

30.2	⊙ RADAR TR ○ Radar Tr	Radar tower	⊚ Radar Tr	
30.3		Radar scanner	⊚ Radar Sc	
30.4	⊙ DOME(RADAR) ⊙ RADOME ○ Dome (Radar) ○ Radome	Radar dome	⊚ Radome	
31	⊙ ANT (RADAR) ○ Ant (Radar)	Dish aerial	⟨	
32	⊙ TANK ⊘ ○ Tk ⊕	Tanks	• ⊕ Tanks	
33	⊙ SILO ⊙ ELEVATOR ○ Silo ○ Elevator	Silo, Elevator	○ Silo ⊚ Silo	Å Å
34.1	ᗐ ⋈	Fortified structure (on large-scale charts)	⸙⸙⸙	
34.2	⯀⯀ Cas	Castle, Fort Blackhouse (on smaller-scale charts)	⯀⯀	✚
34.3	‿⌐	Battery, Small fort (on smaller-scale charts)	⊞	
35.1		Quarry (on large-scale charts)	⸜⸜⸜⸜	
35.2	⚒	Quarry (on smaller-scale charts)	⚒	⚲
36	⚒	Mine	⚒	

Supplementary National Symbols				
a	⚲	Moslem Shrine		
b	⚏	Tomb		

Landmarks

	Watermill		☼
▨ ▸ ▷ Facty	Factory		
○ Well	Well		
■ Sch	School		
■ Hosp	Hospital		
■ Univ	University		
⊙ GAB ○ Gab	Gable		
⚠	Camping site		
Tel Tel Off	Telegraph Telegraph office		
Magz	Magazine		
Govt Ho	Government house		
Inst	Institute		
Ct Ho	Courthouse		
Pav	Pavilion		
T	Telephone		
Ltd	Limited		
Apt	Apartment		
Cap	Capitol		
Co	Company		
Corp	Corporation		

F Ports

		Hydraulic Structures in General	Supplementary national symbols: a—
1		Dike, Levee	
2.1		Seawall (on large-scale charts)	
2.2		Seawall (on smaller-scale charts)	
3	Cswy	Causeway	Causeway
4.1	Bkw	Breakwater (in general)	
4.2		Breakwater (loose boulders, tetrapools, etc.)	
4.3		Breakwater (slope of concrete or masonry)	
5	Training wall	Training wall (partly submerged at high water)	Training wall
6.1	Groin	Groin (always dry)	
6.2	Groin	Groin (intertidal)	
6.3	Groin	Groin (always under water)	

Harbor Installations

	Depths → I	Anchorages, Limits → N	Beacons and other fixed marks → Q	Marina →
10		Fishing harbor		

Ports

2		Mole	
3	Whf	Quay, Wharf	
4	Pier	Pier, Jetty	Pier
5		Promenade pier	Promenade Pier
6		Pontoon	Pontoon
7	Ldg, Lndg	Landing for boats	Lndg
8		Steps, Landing stairs	Steps
9	3 A 3 Ⓐ	Designation of berth	④ Ⓑ
10	Dol Dol (Great Lakes)	Dolphin	Dn.
11		Deviation dolphin	
12	Pile Pile (Great Lakes)	Minor post or pile	
13	Ramp	Slipway, Patent slip, Ramp	Slip
14		Gridiron, Scrubbing grid	Gridiron
15		Dry dock, Graving dock	Dry dock
16		Floating dock	Floating dock
17		Non-tidal basin, Wet dock	
18		Tidal basin, Tidal harbor	

F *Ports*

30		Works on land, with year date		Dock under construction (1996)
31	Under construction (1997)	Works at sea, Area under reclamation, with year date		Area under reclamation (1996)
32	Under constr (1997)	Works under construction, with year date		Under construction (1996) Works in progress (1996)
33.1	Ruins	Ruins		Ru
33.2	Pier	Ruined pier, partly submerged at high water. Submerged ruins		Pier (Ru)
34	Hk	Hulk (actual shape on large scale charts)		Hulk

Canals, Barrages

Clearances → D   Signal Stations → T

40	Canal / Ditch	Canal		km 32 / o km
41.1	Lock / 6 10 6 8 / SPIRE	Lock (on large-scale charts)		Lock
41.2	Canal Lock / Ditch Sluice (Tidegate, Floodgate)	Lock (on smaller-scale charts)		
42		Caisson		
43		Flood barrage		Flood barrage
44		Dam		Dam

Ports

Transhipment Facilities

Supplementary national symbol : d

Roads → D		Railways → D	Tanks → E
	RoRo	Roll-on, Roll-off Ferry (Ro Ro Terminal)	RoRo
		Transit shed. Warehouse (with designation)	2 3 / 2 3
⊖		Timber yard	⌗
⊖	⊖ (4t)	Crane with lifting capacity, crane (on railway)	(3 t)
⊖	⊖ (14t)	Container crane with lifting capacity	(50 t)
		Sheerlegs (conspicuous)	SHEERLEGS

Public Buildings

Supplementary national abbreviation : e

Hbr Mr	Harbormaster's office	⊕
■ Cus Ho	Customhouse	⊖
⊕ Health Office	Health officer's office	⊕
■ Hosp	Hospital	⊕ Hospital
■ PO	Post office	✉

Supplementary National Symbols

	Jetty (partly below MHW)	
	Submerged jetty	
	Jetty (small scale)	
℗	Pump-out facilities	
⊕ Quar	Quarantine	

G *Topographic Terms*

Coast

1	Island	8	Head, Headland
2	Islet	9	Point
3	Cay	10	Spit
4	Peninsula	11	Rock
5	Archipelago	12	Salt marsh, Saltings
6	Atoll	13	Lagoon
7	Cape		

Natural Inland-Features

20	Promontory	30	Plateau
21	Range	31	Valley
22	Ridge	32	Ravine, Cut
23	Mountain, Mount	33	Gorge
24	Summit	34	Vegetation
25	Peak	35	Grassland
26	Volcano	36	Paddy field
27	Hill	37	Bushes
28	Boulder	38	Deciduous woodland
29	Table-land	39	Coniferous woodland

Settlements

50	City, Town	53	Farm
51	Village	54	Saint
52	Fishing village		

Buildings

60	Structure	62	Hut
61	House		

Topographic Terms

Multi-story building		82	Cement works	
Castle		83	Water mill	
Pyramid		84	Greenhouse	
Column		85	Warehouse, Storehouse	
Mast		86	Cold store. Refrigeration storage house	
Lattice tower		87	Refinery	
Mooring mast		88	Power station	
Floodlight		89	Electric works	
Town hall		90	Gas works	
Office		91	Water works	
Observatory		92	Sewage works	
Institute		93	Machine house, Pump house	
Cathedral		94	Well	
Monastery, Convent		95	Telegraph Office	
Lookout station, Watch tower		96	Hotel	
Navigation school		97	Sailors' home	
Naval college		98	Spa hotel	
Factory				
Brick kiln, Brick works				

Road, Rail and Air Traffic

0	Street, Road	116	Runway	
1	Avenue	117	Landing lights	
2	Tramway	118	Helicopter landing site	
3	Viaduct			
4	Suspension bridge			
5	Footbridge			

Ports, Harbors

0	Tidal barrier	132	Loading canal	
1	Boat lift, Ship lift, Hoist	133	Sluice	

G *Topographic Terms*

134	*Basin*	147	*Commercial port, Trade port*
135	*Reservoir*	148	*Building harbor*
136	*Reclamation area*	149	*Oil harbor*
137	*Port*	150	*Ore harbor*
138	*Harbor*	151	*Grain harbor*
139	*Haven*	152	*Container harbor*
140	*Inner harbor*	153	*Timber harbor*
141	*Outer harbor*	154	*Coal harbor*
142	*Deep water harbor*	155	*Ferry harbor*
143	*Free port*	156	*Police*
144	*Customs harbor*		
145	*Naval port*		
146	*Industrial harbor*		

Harbor Installations

170	*Terminal*	185	*Liquefied Natural Gas LNG*
171	*Building slip*	186	*Liquefied Petroleum Gas LPG*
172	*Building yard*	187	*Very Large Crude Carrier VLCC*
173	*Buoy yard, Buoy dump*		
174	*Bunker station*		
175	*Reception facilities for oily wastes*		
176	*Tanker cleaning facilities*		
177	*Cooling water intake/outfall*		
178	*Floating barrier Boom*		
179	*Piling*		
180	*Row of piles*		
181	*Bollard*		
182	*Conveyor*		
183	*Storage tanker*		
184	*Lighter Aboard Ship-LASH*		

Tides, Currents

Supplementary national symbols: a-k

	Chart Datum, Datum for sounding reduction	CD
	Lowest Astronomical Tide	LAT
	Highest Astronomical Tide	HAT
MLW	Mean Low Water	MLW
MHW	Mean High Water	MHW
MSL	Mean Sea Level	MSL
	Land survey datum	
MLWS	Mean Low Water Springs	MLWS
MHWS	Mean High Water Springs	MHWS
MLWN	Mean Low Water Neaps	MLWN
MHWN	Mean High Water Neaps	MHWN
MLLW	Mean Lower Low Water	MLLW
MHHW	Mean Higher High Water	MHHW
	Mean Higher Low Water	MHLW
	Mean Lower High Water	MLHW
Sp	Spring Tide	Sp
Np	Neap tide	Np

H   Tides, Currents

Tidal Levels and charted Data

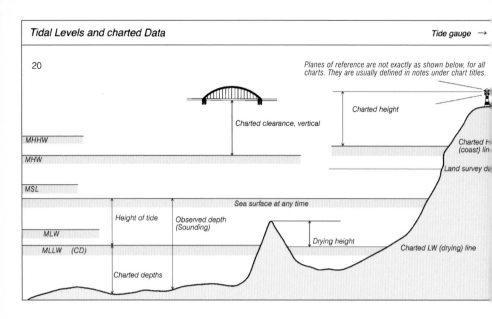

20

Planes of reference are not exactly as shown below, for all charts. They are usually defined in notes under chart titles.

Charted height

Charted clearance, vertical

MHHW

Charted H
(coast) lin

MHW

Land survey da

MSL

Sea surface at any time

Height of tide

Observed depth
(Sounding)

MLW

Drying height

MLLW   (CD)

Charted LW (drying) line

Charted depths

Tide Tables

Tidal Levels referred to Datum of Soundings

Tabular statement of semi-diurnal or diurnal tides

Place	Lat	Long	Heights in meters above datum			
	N/S	E/W	MHWS	MHWN	MLWN	MLWS
30						
			MHHW	MLHW	MHLW	MLLW

Note:
The order of the columns of levels will be the same as that used in national tables of tidal predictions.

31

Tidal streams referred to ..

Tidal stream table

Tidal streams referred to ..

Tides, Currents

'idal Streams and Currents		*Supplementary national symbols:* m-t	
reakers → K		Tide Gauge → T	
2 kn	Flood stream (current) with rate	2.5 kn	
2 kn	Ebb stream (current) with rate	2.5 kn	
	Current in restricted waters		
	Ocean current with rates and seasons	2.5–4.5 kn Jan–Mar (see Note)	
Tide rips — Symbol used only in small areas	Overfalls, tide rips, races		
Eddies — Symbol used only in small areas	Eddies		
Ⓐ Ⓑ	Position of tabulated tidal data with designation	Ⓐ	

upplementary National Symbols		
HW	High water	
HHW	Higher high water	
LW	Low water	
LWD	Low-water datum	
LLW	Lower low water	
MTL	Mean tide level	
ISLW	Indian spring low water	
HWF&C	High-water full and change (vulgar establishment of the port)	
LWF&C	Low-water full and change	

H   *Tides, Currents*

j	CRD	Columbia River Datum	
k	GCLWD	Gulf Coast Low Water Datum	
l	Str	Stream	
m	→2kn→	Current, general, with rate	
n	vel	Velocity; Rate	
o	kn	Knots	
p	ht	Height	
q	fl	Flood	
r	●	New moon	
s	☺	Full moon	
t	(compass diagram)	Current diagram	

Depths

ED	Existence doubtful	ED
SD	Sounding doubtful	SD
Rep	Reported, but not surveyed	Rep
⟨3⟩ Rep (1983)	Reported with year of report, but not surveyed	Rep (1973)
⟨3⟩ Rep	Reported but not confirmed sounding or danger	⟨184⟩ ⟨212⟩

undings

Supplementary national symbols: a - c

Plane of Reference for Depths → H   Plane of Reference for Heights → H

19 8₂ 6¼ / 8₂ 19	19 8₂ 6¾	Sounding in true position (NOS uses upright soundings on English unit charts and sloping soundings on Metric charts).	12 9₇
(23)	⋅— 1036	Sounding out of position	+ (12) 3375
	(5)	Least depth in narrow channel	(9₇)
65̄		No bottom found at depth shown	2̄00
8₂ 19 / 8₂ 19	8₂ 19	Soundings which are unreliable or taken from a smaller-scale source (NOS uses sloping soundings on English unit charts and upright soundings on Metric charts).	12 9₇
6		Drying heights above chart datum	4₉ 0₉ 4₇ 3₈ / 3₈

I Depths

	Depths in Fairways and Areas		Supplementary national symbols: a, ▌
	Plane of Reference for Depths → H		
20	[dashed rectangle outline]	Limit of dredged area	[dashed line]
21	7.0 m	Dredged channel or area with depth of dredging in meters	7.0 m / 7.0 meters
22	24 FEET OCT 1983 / 30 FEET APR 1984	Dredged channel or area with depth and year of the latest control survey	Dredged to 7.2m (1978) / 7.2m (197
23	Maintained depth 7.2m	Dredged channel or area with maintained depth	Maintained depth 7.2m / 7.2m
24	29 23 3 / 30 22 8 / 21 18 7	Depth at chart datum, to which an area has been swept by wire drag. The latest date of sweeping may be shown in parentheses	10_8 / 10_2 / 9_6 (1980) / 11 / 9_8
25	Sand and mud / Unsurveyed / 11 13 17 / 12 10 13 22 rky 20	Unsurveyed or inadequately surveyed area; area with inadequate depth information	Inadequately Surveyed (see Note) / Inadequately Surveyed (see Note)

Depths

epth Contours

Feet	Fm/Meters					
0	0				Low water line	
6	1					
12	2					
18	3					
24	4					
30	5					
36	6				One or two lighter blue tints may	
60	10				be used instead of the 'ribbons'	
120	20				of tint at 10 or 20 m	
180	30					
240	40					
300	50					
600	100					
1,200	200					
1,800	300					
2,400	400					
3,000	500					
6,000	1,000					

Approximate depth contour Continuous lines, with values	— — — — — — —5— (blue or black) —100—	Approximate depth contours	— — —20— — — — — —50— — —

Note: The extent of the blue tint varies with the scale and purpose of the chart, or its sources.
On some charts, contours and figures are printed in blue.

pplementary National Symbols

_ _ _ _ _ _ _ _ _ 6 _ _ _ _ _	Swept channel	
89 17 119 15	Swept area, not adequately sounded (shown by purple or green tint)	
2 ft 6 5	Stream	

J   *Nature of the Seabed*

Types of Seabed

Rocks → K   Supplementary national abbreviations: **a**—

1	S	Sand	S
2	M	Mud	M
3	Cy; Cl	Clay	Cy
4	Sl	Silt	Si
5	St	Stones	St
6	G	Gravel	G
7	P	Pebbles	P
8	Cb	Cobbles	Cb
9	Rk; rky	Rock; Rocky	R
10	Co	Coral and Coraline algae	Co
11	Sh	Shells	Sh
12	S/M	Two layers, e.g. Sand over mud	S/M
13.1	Wd	Weed (including Kelp)	Wd
13.2	⟶ Kelp	Kelp, Seaweed	
14	⟋⟋ Sandwaves	Mobile bottom (sand waves)	
15	⟙ Spring	Freshwater springs in seabed	⟙

Types of Seabed, Intertidal Areas

20	Gravel	Area with stones, gravel or shingle	G St
21	Rock	Rocky area, which covers and uncovers	
22	Coral	Coral reef, which covers and uncovers	

Nature of the Seabed

f; fne	fine	f
m	medium · only used in relation to sand	m
c; crs	coarse	c
bk; brk	broken	bk
sy; stk	sticky	sy
so; sft	soft	so
stf	stiff	sf
Vol	volcanic	v
Ca	calcareous	ca
h; hrd	hard	h

Supplementary National Abbreviations

Grd		Ground	
Oz		Ooze	
Ml		Marl	
Sn		Shingle	
Blds		Boulders	
Ck		Chalk	
Qz		Quartz	
Sch		Schist	
Co Hd		Coral head	
Mds		Madrepores	
Vol Ash		Volcanic ash	
La		Lava	
Pm		Pumice	
T		Tufa	
Sc		Scoriae	
Cn		Cinders	
Mn		Manganese	
Oys		Oysters	
Ms		Mussels	
Spg		Sponge	
K		Kelp	
Grs		Grass	
Stg		Sea-tangle	
Spi		Spicules	
Fr		Forminifera	
Gl		Globigerina	
Di		Diatoms	

J   Nature of the Seabed

ab	Rd		Radiolaria	
ac	Pt		Pteropods	
ad	Po		Polyzoa	
ae	Cir		Cirripedia	
af	Fu		Fucus	
ag	Ma		Mattes	
ah	smi		Small	
ai	lrg		Large	
aj	rt		Rotten	
ak	str		Streaky	
al	spk		Speckled	
am	gty		Gritty	
an	dec		Decayed	
ao	fly		Flinty	
ap	glac		Glacial	
aq	ten		Tenacious	
ar	wh		White	
as	bl; bk		Black	
at	vi		Violet	
au	bu		Blue	
av	gn		Green	
aw	yl		Yellow	
ax	or		Orange	
ay	rd		Red	
az	br		Brown	
ba	ch		Chocolate	
bb	gy		Gray	
bc	lt		Light	
bd	dk		Dark	
be	vard		Varied	
bf	unev		Uneven	

Rocks, Wrecks, Obstructions

General

1	(danger line symbols)	Danger line, in general	(dashed line) ○	
2	21, Rk 21, Obstn (3₂) (3₂) ○₅	Swept by wire drag or diver	└─┘	

Rocks

Plane of Reference for Heights → H   **Plane of Reference for Depths → H**

10	(25) •(21)		Rock (islet) which does not cover, height above height datum	(symbols) (3.1) (1.7)	▲ (4 m)
11	*(2) (2) (4)	*(Q₆) Uncov 2ft (Q₆) Uncov 2ft (1₂)	Rock which covers and uncovers, height above chart datum	(2₇) *(1₆) *(1₆)	◉ ◉
12	* ◉		Rock awash at the level of chart datum	* ◉ ◉	◉
13	+ ◈		Dangerous underwater rock of uncertain depth	+ ◈ ◈	
14		27 Rk	Dangerous underwater rock of known depth	+(4₈) +(12₁)	
14.1	12 Rk	27 R	in the corresponding depth area		
14.2	◈ Rk	(4₂) Rk (4₂) R	outside the corresponding depth area	◈ (4₈) ◈ (12₁)	(3₂)

K   Rocks, Wrecks, Obstructions

15	+ 35 Rk	35 Rk 35 R	Non-dangerous rock, depth known	21 R	35 R. 35 R + (
16	+ Co + 3₁ +	Reef line. +++	Coral reef which covers	Co ++++ Co	
17	Breakers	Br	Breakers		19 5₈ Br 18

Wrecks

Plane of Reference for Depths → H

20	⬭ Hk			Wk	
21	⬭ Hk		Wreck, covers and uncovers, on large-scale charts	Wk	Wk / Wk / Wk / Wk
22			Submerged wreck, depth known, on large-scale charts	5₂ Wk	9 Wk
23		⬭ Hk	Submerged wreck, depth unknown on large-scale charts	Wk	Wk / Wk
24			Wreck showing any portion of hull or superstructure at level of chart datum		Wk / Wk / Wk
25	Masts / Mast (10 ft) Funnel	Masts	Wreck showing mast or masts above chart datum only	Mast	
26	5₁ Wk	5₂ Wk	Wreck, least depth known by sounding only	4₆ Wk 25 Wk	(9)
27	.21. Wk 5 Wk	4₆ Wk	Wreck, least depth known, swept by wire drag or diver	4₆ Wk 25 Wk	.21. F
28			Dangerous wreck, depth unknown		
29			Sunken wreck, not dangerous to surface navigation		
30	8 Wk	25 Wk	Wreck, least depth unknown, but considered to have a safe clearance to the depth shown	25 Wk	15

Rocks, Wrecks, Obstructions

	⬭ Foul # ⌐ F o u l ⌐		Foul ground, non-dangerous to navigation but to be avoided by vessels anchoring, trawling etc.	# ⌐ F o u l ⌐ ⌐ # / ⌐ FB
2	⬭Foul⬭ ⬭Wks⬭ ⬭Wreckage⬭		Foul area. Foul with rocks or wreckage, dangerous to navigation.	

Obstructions

Plane of Reference for Depths → H   Kelp, Sea-Weed → J

	⬭ Obstn	⬭ Obstn	Obstruction, depth unknown	⬭ Obstn Obstn	#
	(5½) Obstn	(5₂) Obstn	Obstruction, least depth known	(4₈) Obstn (16₈) Obstn	
	(21) Obstn (5) Obstn	(4₈) Obstn	Obstruction, least depth known, swept by wire drag or diver	(4₈) Obstn (16₈) Obstn	
1	• • Subm ⊥ Stakes, piles Perches	⬭Obstn ⊺ ⊺ ⊺	Stumps of posts or piles, all or part of the time submerged	⬭ Obstn ⊺ ⊺ ⊺	⊺ Ⓣ Subm piles
2	•• Snags •• Deadhead	•• Stumps	Submerged pile, stake, snag, well, deadhead or stump (with exact position)	Ỉ	⊺ ⊺ ⊺⊺
1	⊔⊔⊔⊔⊔⊔⊔⊔⊔⊔ Fsh stks		Fishing stakes	⊔⊔⊔ ⊔⊔⊔	
2	▯ ⸳⸳⸳⸳ (	⬭	Fish trap, fish weirs, funny nets	⬭	
	— —	⌐ Fish traps ⌐ ⌐ Tunny nets ⌐	Fish trap area, funny nets area	⌐ Fish traps ⌐ ⌐ Tunny nets ⌐	
1	⬭ Obstruction (fish haven) ⊠ (actual shape)	⬭ Obstn (fish haven) ⌐ ⌐ ⊠	Fish haven (artificial fishing reef)	⊠ ⬭	
2	⌐ Obstn ⌐ Fish haven (Auth min 42ft) ⊠	⊠	Fish haven with minimum depth	⊠ (2₄) ⬭ 2₄	
	⬭ Oys ⬭		Shellfish cultivation (stakes visible)	⌐ Shellfish Beds ⌐ ⌐ (see Note) ⌐	

K   *Rocks, Wrecks, Obstructions*

Supplementary National Symbols

a	∗ ✳		Rock awash (height unknown)		
b	5ː Rk 5 Rks		Shoal sounding on isolated rock or rocks		9 R 2 2 P ⊕
c	┽┼┾		Sunken wreck covered 20 to 30 meters		┈┽┼┾┈
d	◌ Sub vol		Submarine volcano		
e	◌ Discol water		Discolored water		
f	21, Rk 3ₓ 3ₓ		Sunken danger with depth cleared (swept) by wire drag		Obstn 21
g	Reef		Reef of unknown extent		
h	◌ ✳Co	Coral Co Co ✳ Co	Coral reef, detached (uncovers at sounding datum)		
i	▱ Subm Crib	▱ Crib	Submerged Crib		▫
j	▢ Crib	▪ Duck Blind	Crib, Duck Blind (above water)		
k	▱ Duck Blind		Submerged Duck Blind		
l	▱ Platform		Submerged Platform		

Offshore Installations

Offshore Installations				
General				
Areas, Limits → N				
		DURRAH OILFIELD	Name of oilfield or gasfield	Oil field	
	⊟ ■ "Hazel"	⊡ "Hazel"	Platform with designation/name	⊡ Z-44	
			Limit of safety zone around offshore installation		
			Limited of development area		

Platforms and Moorings				
Mooring Buoys → Q				
0	■ "Exxon MP-236"	⊡ ⊡	Production platform, Platform, Oil derrick	⊡	
1			Flare stack (at sea)	⊡ Fla	
2		⊡ SPM	Mooring tower, Articulated Loading Platform (ALP). Single Anchor Leg Mooring (SALM)	⊡ SPM	
3	■ "Hazel"	⊡ "Tuna"	Observation/research platform (with name)		
4			Disused platform		
5	⬭ Artificial Island (Mukluk)		Artificial island		
6	⬠		Oil or Gas installation buoy, Catenary Anchor Leg Mooring (CALM), Single Buoy Mooring (SBM)	⬠	
7	⬠	⬠ Tanker	Moored storage tanker		

L *Offshore Installations*

Underwater Installations

Plane of Reference for Depths → H				Obstructions →
20	Well ⊛ (cov 21ft) Well • (cov 83ft) ✦ ✦	⊙ Well	Submerged production well	⊙ Prod. Well
21.1	⊛ Pipe	⊙ Well	Suspended well. depth over wellhead unknown	⊙ Well
21.2	Pipe ⊛ (cov 24ft) Pipe • (cov 92ft)	⟨15⟩ Well	Suspended well, with depth over wellhead	⟨15⟩ Well
21.3			Wellhead with height above the bottom	⊙ Well (5.7)
22			Site of cleared platform	♯
23	• Pipe		Above water wellheads	❯ ⊙ Pipe

Submarine Cables

30.1	∿∿∿∿∿∿	Submarine cable	∿∿∿∿∿∿∿
30.2	Cable Area ┬┬∿∿┬┬ ┴┴∿∿┴┴	Submarine cable area	┬ ┬ ┬ ┬∿∿∿∿┬ ┬ ┬ ┬ ┴ ┴ ┴ ┴∿∿∿∿┴ ┴ ┴ ┴
31.1	∿∿ʃ∿∿ʃ∿∿	Submarine power cable	∿∿∿∿ʃ∿∿∿∿
31.2		∿∿┬ ┬ ┬∿∿ʃ∿∿┬ ∿∿┴ ┴ ┴∿∿ʃ∿∿┴	Submarine power cable area	∿∿┬ ┬ ┬∿∿ʃ∿∿┬ ┬ ┬∿∿ ∿∿┴ ┴ ┴∿∿ʃ∿∿┴ ┴ ┴∿∿
32	∿ ∿ ∿ ∿ ∿	Disused submarine cable	∿ ∿ ∿ ∿ ∿

Offshore Installations

Submarine Pipelines

1		Oil, Gas pipeline	Oil (see note) Gas (see note)	
2	Pipeline Area	Oil, Gas pipeline areas	Oil (see note) Gas (see note)	
1	Water Sewer Outfall Intake	Waterpipe, sewer, outfall pipe, intake pipe	Water Sewer Outfall Intake	
2	Pipeline Area	Discharge pipeline areas	Water Sewer Outfall Intake	
		Buried pipeline pipe (with nominal depth to which buried)	Buried 1.6m	
	PWI Depth over Crib 17ft Crib	Potable Water intake, diffuser, or crib	⊚₂ Obstn	
		Disused pipeline/pipe		

Supplementary National Symbol

Well Well Well	Submerged well (buoyed)		

M   *Tracks, Routes*

Tracks

Tracks Marked by Lights → P		Leading Beacons → Q		Supplementary national symbols: a —
1	Lights in line 090°	Leading line (solid line ins fairway)	2 Bns ≠ 270.5° / 2 Bns ≠ 270°30'	
2	Beacons in line 090°	Transit, clearing line	2 Bns ≠ 270°30' / 2 Bns ≠ 270.5°	
3	Lights in line 090°	Recommended track based on a system of fixed marks	2 Bns ≠ 090.5° – 270.5°	—→ > — > / —→ > — >
4	— < — > — / — < — > —	Recommended tracks not based on a system of fixed marks	— — — — — 090.5° – 270.5° / — — — — < — — > — — — —	
5.1	— — > — — > —	One-way track	☆ — — — ☆ — — — / — — — < — — — — — < — — —	
5.2		Two-way track (including a regulation described in a note)	☆ — — — ☆ — — — SEE NOTE / — < — — >SEE NOTE< — — > —	
6	— — < 7m > — — / — — — < 7₃ m > — — —	Track, recommended track with maximum authorized draft stated	— — < 7.0m > — — / — — — — < 7.3m > — — — —	

Routing Measures

Basic Symbols

Supplementary national symbols: d —

10	⟹	Established (mandatory) direction of traffic flow	⟹
11	= = = ⟹	Recommended direction of traffic flow	= = = ⟹
12		Separation zone	
13		Separation zone	
14	RESTRICTED AREA	Limit of restricted area	
15	— — — — —	Maritime limit in general	
16	PRECAUTIONARY AREA ⚠	Precautionary area	⚠ Precautionary Area

Tracks, Routes

Examples of Routing Measures

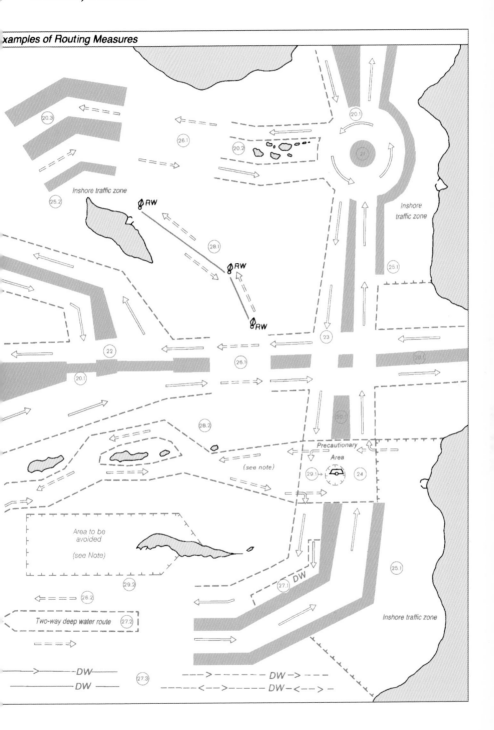

Inshore traffic zone

Inshore traffic zone

RW

RW

RW

Inshore traffic zone

Precautionary Area (see note)

Area to be avoided (see Note)

Two-way deep water route

DW

DW

DW

DW

DW

DW

M *Tracks, Routes*

Examples of Routing Measures

(20.1)	*Traffic separation scheme, traffic separated by separation zone*
(20.2)	*Traffic separation scheme, traffic separated by natural obstructions*
(20.3)	*Traffic separation scheme, with outer separation zone, separating traffic using scheme from traffic not using it*
(21)	*Traffic separation scheme, roundabout*
(22)	*Traffic separation scheme, with "crossing gates"*
(23)	*Traffic separation schemes crossing, without designated precautionary area*
(24)	*Precautionary area*
(25.1)	*Inshore traffic zone, with defined end-limits*
(25.2)	*Inshore traffic zone without defined end-limits*
(26.1)	*Recommended direction of traffic flow, between Traffic separations schemes*
(26.2)	*Recommended direction of traffic flow, for ships not needing a deep water route*
(27.1)	*Deep water route, as part of one-way traffic lane*
(27.2)	*Two-way deep water route, with minimum depth stated*
(27.3)	*Deep water route, centerline as recommended One-way or Two-way track*
(28.1)	*Recommended route (often marked by centerline buoys)*
(28.2)	*Two-way route with one-way sections*
(29.1)	*Area to be avoided, around navigational aid*
(29.2)	*Area to be avoided, because of danger of stranding*

Tracks, Routes

adar Surveillance Systems

⊙ Ra		Radar Surveillance Station	⊚ Radar Surveillance Station	
		Radar range	Ra Cuxhaven	
1		Radar reference line	_____ Ra _____	— Ra ——— Ra —
2		Radar reference line coinciding with a leading line	Ra 270°-090°	

adio Reporting Points

◁(A) ◁(B) ◁(3)	Radio reporting (calling-in or way) points showing direction(s) of vessel movement with designation (if any)	◁ ◁(B) ◁(7)

rries

Ferry Ferry	Ferry	___-_-__-_-_-□-_-_-_-_-_
Cable ferry	Cable Ferry	_-_-_-_-_-_-□-_-_-_-_ Cable Ferry

pplementary National Symbols

←→DW←→	Recommended track for deep draft vessels (track not defined by fixed marks)	
←→DW 83 ft←→ DW 76 ft	Depth is shown where it has been obtained by the cognizant authority	
_ _ _ _ _	Alternate course	
(roundabout symbol)	Established traffic separation scheme: Roundabout	
○	If no separation zone exists, the center of the roundabout is shown by a circle	

Dredged and Swept Areas → I	Submarine Cables, Submarine Pipelines → L	Tracks, Routes →

General

1.1		Maritime limit in general usually implying: Permanent obstructions	
1.2		Maritime limit in general usually implying: No permanent obstructions	
2.1	Restricted Area	Limit of restricted area	
2.2	PROHIBITED AREA — PROHIB AREA	(Screen optional) Limit of prohibited area (no unauthorized entry)	Entry Prohibited

Anchorages, Anchorage Areas

10	⚓ ⚓ ⚓	⚓	Anchorage (large vessels)	⚓	⚓ ⚓ ⚓
		⚓	Anchorage (small vessels)		
11.1	(14)		Anchor berths	(A) N 53 (14)	(6) No1
11.2	3	D17	Anchor berths, swinging circle may be shown	(A) (N 53) (14)	
12.1	– – – – – – –	⚓ Anchorage	Anchorage area in general	⚓ ⚓ ⚓ ⚓	
12.2		Anchorage No 1	Numbered anchorage area	⚓ ⚓ No 1 ⚓	
12.3		Neufeld Anchorage	Named anchorage area	⚓ ⚓ Neufeld ⚓	
12.4		DW Anchprage	Deep Water Anchorage area. Anchorage area for Deep Draft Vessels	⚓ ⚓ DW ⚓	
12.5		Tanker Anchorage	Tanker anchorage area	⚓ ⚓ Tanker ⚓	

Areas, Limits

6		Anchorage for periods up to 24 hours	⚓ - - - - - - - ⚓ 24 h ⚓	
7	Explosives Anchorage	Explosives anchorage area	⚓ - - - - - - - ⚓ - ⚓ ⚓	
8	QUAR ANCH / QUARANTINE ANCHORAGE / Quarantine Anchorage	Quarantine anchorage area	⚓ - - - - - - - ⚓ - ⊕ ⚓	⚓
9		Reserved anchorage	⚓ - - - - - - ⚓ - - Reserved ⚓ (see Caution)	Anch Reserved

Note: Anchors as part of the limit symbol are not shown for small areas. Other types of anchorage areas may be shown.

		Sea-plane landing area		⚓ Y ⚓
		Anchorage for sea-planes	⚓	

Restricted Areas

ANCH PROHIB / Anch Prohibited	ANCH PROHIB	Anchoring prohibited		
Fish Prohibited	FISH PROHIB	Fishing prohibited		
		Limit of nature reserve: Nature reserve, Bird sanctuary, Game preserve, Seal sanctuary		
1	Explosives Dumping Ground	Explosives Dumping Ground	Explosives dumping ground	Explosives Dumping Ground	
2	Explosives Dumping Ground (Discontd)	Explosives Dumping Ground (disused)	Explosives dumping ground (disused) Foul (explosives)	Explosives Dumping Ground (disused)	

24	Dump Site	Dumping Ground	Dumping ground for chemical waste	Dumping Ground for Chemical waste	
25	Degaussing Range	Degaussing Range	Degaussing range	Degaussing range	
26		Historic Wreck (see note)	Historic wreck and restricted area	Historic Wk	

Military Practice Areas

30			Firing danger area		
31	PROHIBITED AREA	Prohibited Area	Military area, entry prohibited	Entry Prohibited	
32			Mine-laying practice area		
33			Submarine transit lane and exercise area		
34			Mine field	Minefield (see Caution)	

International Boundaries and National Limits

Supplementary national symbols: **a,**

40	++++++++	——— -- ———	International boundary on land	DENMARK + + + + + + + + FEDERAL REPUBLIC OF GERMANY	
41	CANADA — + — + — UNITED STATES	— + — + — + —	International maritime boundary	DENMARK + — + — + — FEDERAL REPUBLIC OF GERMANY	
42	▬▬▬▬	——— - - ———	Straight territorial sea baseline		
43	▬▬▬▬	— + — + —	Seaward limit of territorial sea	— + — + —	
44	▬▬▬▬	— + —	Seaward limit of contiguous zone	— + —	

Areas, Limits

–×◇–		Limits of fishery zones	———×◇——— – – –×◇– – –	
		Limit of continental shelf		
–×◇–		Limit of Exclusive Economic Zone	——— EEZ ———	
		Customs limit	– – – –⊖– – – –	– – – –
	Harbor Limit	Harbor limit	Harbour limit	–·–·–·

arious Limits

Supplementary national symbols: c-g

1	⌐‾‾‾‾‾¬	Limit of fast ice, Ice front	⋔⋔⋔⋔⋔⋔	
2	⌐⌐⌐⌐	Limit of sea ice (pack ice)-seasonal	⋔⋔⋔⋔⋔⋔	
	·—Log boom—·	Log pond	Log Pond	|—|——|——
1	Spoil Area	Spoil ground	Spoil Ground	⌐‾‾‾⌐⋀⋀‾‾¬
2	Spoil Area Discontinued	Spoil ground (disused)	Spoil Ground (disused)	
		Dredging area	Dredging Area (see Note)	
		Cargo transhipment area	Cargo Transhipment Area	
		Incineration area	Incineration Area	

pplementary National Symbols

– – – – –		COLREGS demarcation line	
——— · ———		Limit of fishing areas (fish trap areas)	
⌐ ‾ ‾ ¬ Dumping Ground		Dumping ground	

d	Disposal Area 92 depths from survey of JUNE 1972 85	Disposal area (Dump Site)	
e	- - - - - - - - - - - - - - - - - -	Limit of airport	
f	—— · —— —— - ——	Reservation line (Optional)	
g	Dump Site	Dump site	

Hydrographic Terms

Ocean	43		43		Shelf-edge
	Sea		44		Slope
G	Gulf		45		Continental slope
B	Bay, Bayou		46		Continental rise
Fd	Fjord		47		Continental borderland
L	Loch, Lough, Lake		48		Basin
Cr	Creek		49		Abyssal plain
Lag	Lagoon		50		Hole
C	Cove		51		Trench
In	Inlet		52		Trough
Str	Strait		53		Valley
Sd	Sound		54		Median Valley
Pass	Passage, Pass		55		Canyon
Chan	Channel		56		Seachannel
	Narrows		57		Moat, Sea moat
Entr	Entrance		58		Fan
Est	Estuary		59		Apron
	Delta		60		Fracture zone
Mth	Mouth		61		Scarp, Escarpment
Rd	Roads, Roadstead		62		Sill
Arch	Anchorage		63		Gap
Apprs	Approach, Approaches		64		Saddle
Bk	Bank		65		Levee
			66		Province
Shl	Shoal		67		Tideway, Tidal gully
Rf Co rf	Reef, Coral reel		68		Sidearm
	Sunken rock		Other Terms		
Le	Ledge		80		projected
	Pinnacle		81		lighted
	Ridge		82		buoyed
	Rise		83		marked
Mt	Mountain, Mount		84	anc	ancient
	Seamount		85	dist	distant
	Seamount chain		86		lesser
Pk	Peak		87		closed
	Knoll		88		partly
	Abyssal hill		89	approx	approximate
	Tablemount		90	Subm, subm	summerged
	Plateau		91		shoaled
	Terrace		92	exper	experiment
	Spur		93	D. Destr	destroyed
	Continental shelf				

P *Lights*

Light Structures, Major Floating Lights

				Description				
1				Major light, minor light light, lighthouse		Lt Lt Ho		
2	■ PLATFORM (lighted)		⊡	Lighted offshore platform	⊡			
3	○ Marker (lighted)	BY		Lighted beacon tower	BY	Bn Tr		
4		R		Lighted beacon	R	BRB	Bn	
5	○ Art	R		Articulated light Buoyant beacon, resilient beacon	R	Bn		
6				Light vessel; Lightship Normally manned light-vessel				
7				Unmanned light-vessel; light float			FLOAT	
8				LANBY, superbuoy as navigational aid				

Lights

ight Characters on Light Buoys → Q

	Abbreviation		Class of light	Illustration	Period shown ⊢——⊣	
	International	National				
1	F	F	Fixed			F
	Occulting (total duration of light longer than total duration of darkness)					
2	Oc	Oc	Single-occulting			Oc
	Oc(2) Example	Oc (2)	Group-occulting			Oc (2)
	Oc(2+3) Example	Oc(2+3)	Composite group-occulting			Oc(2+3)
	Isophase (duration of light and darkness equal)					
3	Iso	Iso	Isophase			Iso
	Flashing (total duration of light shorter than total duration of darkness)					
4	Fl	Fl	Single-flashing			Fl
	Fl(3) Example	Fl (3)	Group-flashing			Fl (3)
	Fl(2+1) Example	Fl (2+1)	Composite group-flashing			Fl (2+1)
5	LFl	L Fl	Long-flashing (flash 2 s or longer)			L Fl
	Quick (repetition rate of 50 to 79 – usually either 50 or 60 – flashes per minute)					
6	Q	Q	Continuous quick			Q
	Q(3) Example	Q(3)	Group quick			Q
	IQ	IQ	Interrupted quick			IQ

P *Lights*

	Abbreviation		Class of light	Illustration	Period shown ⊢———⊣	
	International	National				
	Very quick (repetition rate of 80 to 159 – usually either 100 or 120 – flashes per min)					
10.7	VQ	VQ	Continuous very quick			VQ
	VQ(3) Example	VQ (3)	Group very quick			
	IVQ	IVQ	Interrupted very quick			
10.8	Ultra quick (repetition rate of 160 or more – usually 240 to 300 – flashes per min)					
	UQ	UQ	Continuous ultra quick			
	IUQ	IUQ	Interrupted ultra quick			
10.9	Mo (A) Example	Mo (A)	Morse Code			
10.10	FFl	F Fl	Fixed and flashing			F Fl
10.11	Al.WR	AIWR	Alternating	R W R W R W		AIWR

Colors of Lights

11.1	W		W		White (only on sector-and alternating lights)	Colors of lights shown on standard charts
11.2	R		R		Red	
11.3	G		G		Green	
11.4	Bu		Bu		Blue	on multicolored charts
11.5	Vi		Vi		Violet	
11.6	Y		Y		Yellow	
11.7	Y	Or	Y	Or	Orange	on multicolored charts at sector lights
11.8	Y	Am	Y	Am	Amber	

Lights

90s		Period in seconds	90s

evation

ane of Reference for Heights → H			Tidal Levels → H
12m 36ft		Elevation of light given in meters or feet	12m

ange

te: Charted ranges are nominal ranges given in Nautical miles

15M	15M	Light with single range	15M
10M	15/10M	Light with two different ranges NOS: only lesser of two ranges in charted	15/10M
7M	15-7M	Light with three or more ranges NOS: only least of three ranges is charted	15-7M

isposition

	(hor)	horizontally disposed	(hor)
	(vert)	vertically disposed	(vert)

xample of a full Light Description

Name
Fl (3) WRG 15s 21ft 11M
Fl (3) WRG 15s 21m 15-11M-NIMA

Fl(3)	Class of light: group flashing repeating a group of three flashes
WRG	Colors: white, red, green, exhibiting the different colors in defined sectors
15S	Period: the time taken to exhibit one full sequence of 3 flashes and eclipses: 15 seconds
21ft 21m	Elevation of local plane above datum: 21 feet or 21 meters
11M 15-11M	Nominal range NIMA: white 15M, green 11M, red between 15 and 11M.

Name
Fl(3)WRG.15s 21m 15-11M

Fl(3)	Class of light: group flashing repeating a group of three flashes
WRG	Colors: white, red, green exhibiting the different colors in defined sectors
15s	Period: the time taken to exhibit one full sequence of 3 flashes and eclipses: 15 seconds
21m	Elevation of local plane above datum: 21 meters
15-11M	Nominal range: white 15M, green 11M, red between 15 and 11M

P   *Lights*

Lights Marking Fairways

Leading Lights and Lights in Line

20.1	![Lts in line 270°]	Leading lights with leading line (firm line is fairway) and arcs of visibility Bearing given in degrees and tenths of a degree	Name Oc.3s 8m 12M Name Oc.6s 24m 15M
20.2		Leading lights ‡: any two objects in line Bearing given in degrees and minutes	Oc.4s 12M Oc.R & Oc ‡ 269° Oc.R 4s 10M
20.3	F Bu, Iso 2s	Leading lights on small-scale charts	Ldg Oc.R & F.R
21		Lights in line, marking the sides of a channel	Fl.G Fl.G 2 Fl.R
22		Rear or upper light	Rear Lt or Upper Lt
23		Front or lower light	Front Lt or Lower Lt

Direction Lights

30.1	RED GREEN	Direction light with narrow sector and course to be followed, flanked by darkness or unintensified light	Dir Fl(2) 5s 10m 11M
30.2		Direction light with course to be followed, uncharted sector is flanked by darkness or unintensified light	Oc.12s 6M Dir 255° Dir 299° Fl(2) 5s 11M
30.3		Direction light with narrow fairway sector flanked by sectors or different character	F.G Al.WR Oc. Dir WRG. 15-5M Al.WR F.R
31		Moiré effect light (day and night) Arrows show when course alteration needed	Dir 295°

Note: Quoted bearings are always from seaward.

Lights

	Sector light on standard charts	Fl.WRG.4s 21m 18-12M
1	Sector lights on standard charts, the white sector limits marking the sides of the fairway	Fl.G.Fl.W.3s Name Oc.WRG. 10-6M Oc.R Oc.W Oc.G Name
2	Sector lights on multicoloured charts, the white sector limits marking the sides of the fairway	Fl.G.Fl.W.3s Name Oc.WRG. 10-6M Oc.R Oc.W Oc.G Name
	Main light visible all-round with red subsidiary light seen over danger	Fl(3) 10s 62m 25M F.R.55m 12M F.R
	All-round light with obscured sector	Fl.5s 41m 30M Obscd
	Light with arc of visibility deliberately restricted	Iso.WRG.
	Light with faint sector	Faint Q.14m 5M
	Light with intensified sector	Oc.R.8s 7M R Intens Oc.R.8s R5M R7M R5M

P   Lights

Lights with limited Times of Exhibition

50	Occas	! FR (occas)	Lights exhibited only when specially needed (for fishing vessels, ferries) and some private lights	☆ F.R. (occas)	
51		F Bu 9m 6M (F by day)	Daytime light (charted only where the character shown by day differs from that shown at night)	Fl.10s 40m 27M ☆ (F.37m 11M Day)	
52			Fog light (exhibited only in fog, or character charges in fog)	Name ☆ Q.WRG.5m 10-3M Fl.5S (in fog)	
53			Unwatched (unmanned) light with no standby or emergency arrangements	☆ Fl.5s (U)	
54			Temporary	(temp)	
55			Extinguished	(exting)	

Special Lights

Flare Stack (at Sea) → L   Flare Stack (on Land) → E   Signal Stations →

60	! AERO	AERO AI WG 7½s 108m 13M	Aero light	✳ Aero Al.Fl.WG.7.5s 11M	★ AERO
61.1		AERO FR 77m 11M	Air obstruction light of high intensity	Aero F.R.313m 11M ✳ RADIO MAST (353)	
61.2		⊙ TR (R Lts)	Air obstruction lights of low intensity	(89) ᵢ (R Lts)	
62		Fog Det Lt	Fog detector light	Fog Det Lt	
63		⬳	Floodlight, floodlighting of a structure	⬳ (Illuminated)	
64			Strip light		
65	! Priv	! F R (priv)	Private light other than one exhibited occasionally	F.R.(priv)	★ ● Priv maint

Supplementary National Symbols

a	❂		Riprap surrounding light		
b			Short-Long Flashing		S-L Fl
c			Group-Short Flashing		▲▲ ▲▲ ▲▲
d			Fixed and Group Flashing		F Gp Fl

Buoys, Beacons

Buoys and Beacons

IALA Maritime Buoyage System, which includes Beacons → Q 130

o	⊶	Position of buoy	⊶

Colors of Buoys and Beacon Topmarks

Abbreviations for Colors → P

			Description	
G			Green and black	B, G, B, G, G, G
R		R, Y, R	Single colors other than green and black	R, R, Y, Y, R
RG		BY, GRG	Multiple colors in horizontal bands, the color sequence is from top to bottom	BY, GRG, BRB
		RW, RW	Multiple colors in vertical or diagonal stripes, the darker color is given first	RW, RW, RW
			Retroreflecting material	

Retroreflecting material may be fitted to some unit marks. Charts do not usually show it. Under IALA Recommendations, black bands will appear blue under a spotlight.

Lighted Marks

Marks with Fog Signals → R

		Description	
	Fl R (R), Fl.G (G)	Lighted marks on standard charts	Fl.G (G), Fl.R (R)
		Lighted marks on multicolored charts	Fl.R (R), Iso (RW), Fl.G (G)

Topmarks and Radar Reflectors

For Application of Topmarks within the IALA-System → Q 130   Topmarks on Special Purpose Buoys and Beacons → Q

		Description	
(topmarks)	(topmarks)	IALA System buoy topmarks (beacon topmarks shown upright)	(topmarks)
	No 2 (R)	Beacon with topmark, color, radar reflector and designation	No 2 Name (R)
	No 3 (G)	Buoy with topmark, color, radar reflector and designation	No 3 (G)

Note: Radar reflectors on floating marks are usually not charted.

Q   Buoys, Beacons

Buoys   Features Common to Buoys and Beacons → Q 1–11

Shapes of Buoys

20	β N △	△	Conical buoy, nun buoy	△	
21	β C ◻	◻	Can or cylindrical buoy	◻	
22	β SP ◠	◠	Spherical buoy	◠	
23	β P ⏁	⏁	Pillar buoy	⏁	
24	β S ⌿	⌿	Spar buoy, spindle buoy	⌿	
25	β ◠	◠	Barrel buoy	◠	
26	⏛	⏛	Super buoy	⏛	

Light Floats

| 30 | ⚓ | ⚓ Fl G 3s Name | Light float as part of IALA System | ⚓ Fl.G.3s No 3 Name | ⚓ |
| 31 | | ⛴ Fl(2) 10s 11M | Light float (unmarked light-vessel) not part of IALA System | ⛴ Fl.10s 12m 26M | |

Mooring Buoys

Oil or Gas Installation Buoy → L   Small Craft Mooring → ▪

40	➤		Mooring buoys	⚓ ⚓ ⚓ ⚓	
41	➤	➤ Fl Y 2s	Lighted mooring buoy (example)	⚓ Fl.Y.2.5s	
42			Trot, mooring buoys with ground tackle and berth numbers	⚓–①–⚓–②–⚓	
43	See Supplementary national symbols m,n		Mooring buoy with telegraphic or telephonic communication	⚓〰〰〰〰	
44		➤ (5 buoys) Moorings	Numerous moorings (example)	⌐ Small Craft Moorings ¬	

Buoys, Beacons

ecial Purpose Buoys

e. *Shapes of buoys are variable. Lateral or Cardinal buoys may be used in some situations.*

		Firing danger area (Danger Zone) buoy	⚲ DZ
		Target	⚲ Target
		Marker Ship	⚲ Marker Ship
		Barge	⚲ Barge
		Degaussing Range buoy	⚲
⚲ Tel		Cable buoy	⚲
⚲		Spoil ground buoy	⚲
⚲		Buoy marking outfall	⚲
⚲ ODAS		ODAS-buoy/Ocean-Data-Acquisition System). Data-Collecting buoy of superbuoy size	⚲ ODAS
⚲ w or ✝ ⚲ ⚲ w or △ ⚲		Special-purpose buoys	
		Wave recorder, current master	⚲
⚲ AERO		Seaplane anchorage buoy	
		Buoy marking traffic separation scheme	
		Buoy marking recreation zone	⚲

asonal Buoys

⚲ Priv	(maintained by private interests, use with caution)	Buoy privately maintained (example)	⚲ (priv)
		Seasonal buoy (example)	⚲ (Apr – Oct)

Q *Buoys, Beacons*

Beacons

Lighted Beacons → P   Features Common to Beacons and Buoys → Q 1–

80	☐ Bn	⚓ ⊙ Bn	Beacon in general, characteristics unknown or chart scale too small to show	⚓ ⊙ Bn
81	☐ RW ▲ ▣	⚓ BW	Beacon with color, no distinctive topmark	⚓ BW
82		⚓ R ⚓ BY	Beacons with colors and topmarks (example)	⚓ R ⚓ BY ⚓ BRB
83			Beacon on submerged rock (topmark as appropriate)	⚓ BRB ⚓ BRB

Minor impermanent Marks usually in drying Areas (Lateral Mark of Minor Channel)

Minor Pile → F

				PORT HAND	STARBOARD H
90	● Pole ● Pole	⊥	Stake. Pole	⊥	
91	● Stake ● Stake	⊥	Perch. Stake	Υ	↑
92			Withy	⚏	⚏

Minor Marks, usually on Land

Landmarks → E

100	⊙CAIRN °Cairn	⊙CAIRN °Cairn ⚘	Cairn	⚘
101			Colored or white mark	☐ Mk

Beacon Towers

110	☐ RW	⬠ R ⬠ G ⬠ R ⬠ G	Beacon towers without and with topmarks and colors (example)	⬠ R ⬠ G ⬠ R ⬠ G ⬠ BY ⬠ BRB
111			Lattice beacon	⬠

Buoys, Beacons

aing Lines, Clearing Lines → M

e. Topmarks and colors shown where scale permits.

	Bns in line 270°	Leading beacons	
	Bns in line 270°	Beacons marking a clearing line	
COURSE 270°00' TRUE MARKERS MARKERS		Beacons marking measured distance with quoted bearings	Measured Distance 1852m 090°- 270
	W	Cable landing beacon (example)	
		Refuge beacon	Ref. Ref.
		Firing danger area beacons	
		Notice board	

Q   *Buoys, Beacons*

---

130 *IALA Maritime Buoyage System*

IALA   International Association of Lighthouse Authorities

Where in force, the IALA System applies to all fixed and floating marks except lighthouses, sector lights, leading lights and leading marks, light-vessels and lanby
The standard buoy shapes are cylindrical (can) ⌑ , conical △ , spherical ⌒ , pillar ⌰ , and spar ⌶ , but variations may occur, for example: light-floats ⇨
In the illustrations below, only the standard buoy shapes are used. In the case of fixed beacons (lit or unlit) only the shape of the topmark is of navigational significance

---

130.1 *Lateral marks* are generally for well-defined channels. There are two international Buoyage Regions – A and B – where Lateral marks di

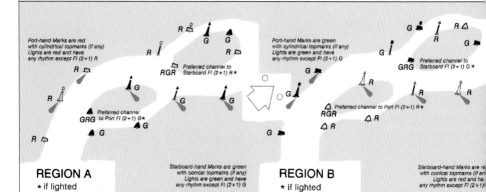

Port-hand Marks are red
with cylindrical topmarks (if any)
Lights are red and have
any rhythm except Fl (2+1) R

Preferred channel to
Starboard Fl (2+1) R ★

Preferred channel
GRG to Port Fl (2+1) G★

REGION A
★ if lighted

Starboard-hand Marks are green
with conical topmarks (if any)
Lights are green and have
any rhythm except Fl (2+1) G

Port-hand Marks are green
with cylindrical topmarks (if any)
Lights are green and have
any rhythm except Fl (2+1) G

Preferred channel to
GRG Starboard Fl (2+1) G ★

Preferred channel to Port Fl (2+1) R★

REGION B
★ if lighted

Starboard-hand Marks are re
with conical topmarks (if an
Lights are red and ha
any rhythm except Fl (2+1)

A preferred channel buoy may also be a pillar or a spar. All preferred channel marks have horizontal bands of color.
Where for exceptional reasons an Authority considers that a green color for buoys is not satisfactory, black may be used.

IALA Buoyage Regions A and B

130.2 *Direction of Buoyage*

The direction and buoyage is that taken when approaching a harbor from seaward or along coasts, the direction determined by buoyage authori
normally clockwise around land masses.
Symbol showing direction of buoyage where not obvious.
Symbol showing direction of buoyage on multicolored charts.

    Symbol showing direction of buoyage where not obvious.

    Symbol showing direction of
buoyage on multicolored charts.

126 CHART NO. 1

Buoys, Beacons

The illustrations below all marks are the same in Regions A and B.

130.3 *Cardinal Marks indicating navigable water to the named side of the marks.*

UNLIT MARKS

Topmark: 2 black cones

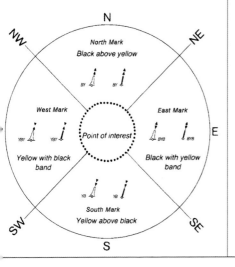

North Mark
Black above yellow

West Mark
Yellow with black band

Point of interest

East Mark
Black with yellow band

South Mark
Yellow above black

LIGHTED MARKS

White Light

Time (seconds)
0   5   10   15

North Mark	N	BY	VQ or Q
East Mark	E	BYB	VQ(3)5s or Q(3)10s
South Mark	S	YB	VQ(6)+LFl 10s or Q(6)+LFl 15s
West Mark	W	YBY	VQ(9)10s or Q(9)15s

The same abbreviations are used for lights on spar buoys and beacons. The periods 5s, 10s and 15s, may not always be charted.

130.4 *Isolated Danger Marks stationed over dangers with navigable water around them.*

Body: black with red horizontal band(s)
Topmark: 2 black spheres

BRB   BRB

BRB   BRB   Fl(2)   white light

130.5 *Safe Water Marks such as mid-channel and landfall marks.*

Body: red and white vertical stripes
Topmark (if any): red sphere

RW   RW   RW

RW   RW   RW   Oc, or Iso, or L Fl 10s, or Mo (A)   white light

---

130.6 *Special Marks not primarily to assist navigation but to indicate special features*

Body (shape optional): yellow ‡
Topmark (if any): yellow X

Y   Y

Y   Y   Y   Fl.Y etc.   yellow light (rhythm optional)

‡ In special cases yellow can be in conjunction with another color.

BEACONS with IALA System topmarks are charted by upright symbols. eg.   minor (beacon)   or, on smaller-scale charts: Bn   Bn

Q *Buoys, Beacons*

Supplementary National Symbols

a	⚲ BELL ⚲ BELL	Bell buoy		
b	⚲ GONG ⚲ GONG	Gong buoy		
c	⚲ WHIS ⚲ WHIS	Whistle buoy		
d	⚲RW	Fairway buoy (RWVS)		
e	⚲RW	Midchannel buoy (RWVS)		
f	⚲ R "2"	Starboard – hand buoy (entering from seaward – US waters)		
g	⚲ "1" ⚲ "1"	Port – hand buoy (entering from seaward – US waters)		
h	⚲BR ⚲RG ⚲GR ⚲G	Bifurcation, Junction, Isolated danger, Wreck and Obstruction buoys		
i	⚲ Y		Fish trap (area) buoy		
j	⚲ Y		Anchorage buoy (marks limits)		
k	B		Black		
l	▲ R Bn △ RG Bn	Triangular shape beacons		
	■G Bn □GR Bn □W Bn □B Bn	Square shaped beacons		
	□Bn	Beacon, color unknown		
m		⬅Tel ⬅Tel	Mooring buoy with telegraphic communications		
n		⬅T ⬅T	Mooring buoy with telephonic communications		
o	⏚		Lighted beacon		! Bn ⚓

Fog Signals

General

Fog Detector Light → P			Fog Light → P
Fog Sig)))	)))	Position of fog signal. Type of fog signal not stated	etc.

Types of Fog Signals, with Abbreviations

Supplementary national symbols: **a**

GUN	Explosive	Explos
DIA	Diaphone	Dia
SIREN	Siren	Siren
HORN	Horn (nautophone, reed, tylon)	Horn
BELL	Bell	Bell
WHIS	Whistle	Whis
GONG	Gong	Gong

Examples of Fog Signal Descriptions

Fl 3s 70m 29M SIREN Mo(N) 60s	Fl 3s 70m 29M SIREN	Siren at a lighthouse, giving a long blast followed by a short one (N), repeated every 60 seconds	Fl.3s 70m 29M Siren Mo(N)60S ‡
BELL	BELL	Wave-actuated bell buoy	Bell ‡
Q(6)+LFl 15s HORN(1) 15s WHIS	Q(6)+LFl 15s HORN WHIS	Light buoy, with horn giving a single blast every 15 seconds, in conjunction with a wave-actuated whistle	Q(6)+LFl.15s Horn(1) 15s Whis ‡
‡	The fog signal symbol may be omitted when a description of the signal is given.		

R   *Fog Signals*

Supplementary National Symbols				
a	Mo		*Morse Code fog signal*	

Radar, Radio, Electronic Position-Fixing Systems

Radar

Radar Structures Forming Landmarks → E		Radar Surveillance Systems → M
⊙ Ra	Coast radar station, providing range and bearing service on request	⊚ Ra
⊙ Ramark	Ramark, radar beacon transmitting continuously	⊚ Ramark
⊙ RACON	Radar transporter beacon, with morse identification, responding within the 3-cm (X-)band	⊚ Racon(Z)
	Radar transponder beacon, with morse identification, responding within the 10-cm (S-)band	⊚ Racon(Z) (10cm)
	Radar transponder beacon, responding within the 3-cm(X-) and the 10-cm (S-)band	⊚ Racon(Z) (3&10cm)
	Radar transponder beacon, responding on a fixed frequency outside the marine band	⊚ F Racon
	Radar transponder beacons with bearing line	⊚ ⊚ Racons ⊥ 270° Racon Racon
RACON (−) R "2" FI R 4s Racon	Floating marks with radar transponder beacons	Racon Racon
Ra Ref	Radar reflector	
Ra (conspic)	Radar-conspicuous feature	

Radio

Radio Structures Forming Landmarks → E		Radio Reporting (Calling-in or Way) Points → M
⊙ R Bn, RC	Circular (non-directional) marine or aeromarine radiobeacon	⊚ Name RC
⊙ RD 072°30′ RD	Directional radiobeacon with bearing line	RD ⊚ RD 269.5°
⊙ RW	Rotating-pattern radiobeacon	⊚ RW

13	⊙ CONSOL Bn 190 kHz MMF ▆▆.	⊚ CONSOL	*Consol beacon*	⊙ Consol
14	⊙ RDF		*Radio direction-finding station*	⊙ RG
15	○ R Sta	⊚ R	*Coast radio station providing QTG service*	⊙ R
16	⊙ AERO R Bn		*Aeronautical radiobeacon*	⊙ Aero R C

Electronic Position-Fixing Systems

Decca

20		AB AC AD	*Identification of Lattice Patterns*	**AB**	AC	AD
21		——————	*Line of Position (LOP)*	———————		
22			*Line of Position representing Zone Limit (or. On larger scales) other intermediate LOPs*	———————		
23			*Half-lane LOP*	— — — — —		
24			*LOP from adjoining Chain (on Interchain Fixing Charts)*	— — — — —		
25		A 12	*Lane value. With Chain designator (Interchain Charts only) and Zone designator*	(6) A 12		

Note: A Decca Chain Coverage Diagram is given when patterns from more than one Chain appear on a chart. LOPs are normally theoretical ones: if Fixed Error is included, an explanatory note is given.

Loran-C

30	9960–Y	9960–Z	*Identification of Loran-C-Rates*	7970–X
31	———————		*Line of Position (LOP)*	———————
32			*LOP representing time difference value of an integral thousand ||s (microsecond)*	———————
33			*LOP beyond reliable groundwave service area*	— — — —

Radar, Radio, Electronic Position-Fixing Systems

4		LOP from adjoining Chain	– – – – – – – –
5		LOP from adjoining Chain beyond reliable groundwave service area	– – – – – – – – –
6	9960–Z–58000	LOP labeled with rate and full us value	7970–X 33000
7	050	LOP labeled with final three digits only	050

ote: A Loran-C Chain Diagram may be given if rates from more than one Chain appear in a chart.
And explanatory note is given if LOPs include propagation delays.

Omega

0	DF **CF** AC		Charted station pairs	AB BC
1	———————————		Line of Position (LOP)	———————————
2	DF - 702		Lane values	897 AB–900

ote: A cautionary note draws attention to the need to consult Propagation Prediction Correction (PPC) tables.
An explanatory note draws attention to the unreliability of LOPs within 450 n miles of a transmitter.

Satellite Navigation Systems

0	WGS WGS 72 WGS **84**	World Geodetic System. 1972 or 1984	WGS WGS 72 WGS **84**

ote: A note may be shown to indicate the sifts of latitude and longitude in hundredths of a minute. Which should be made to satellite-derived
positions (which are referred to WGS) to relate them to the chart.

T Services

Pilotage

1.1	Pilots ⓘ	ⓘ	Boarding place, position of a Pilot-Cruising Vessel	ⓘ
1.2		ⓘ Name	Boarding place, position of a Pilot-Cruising Vessel, with name (e. g. District, Port)	ⓘ Name
1.3		ⓘ (see note)	Boarding place, position of a Pilot-Cruising Vessel, with note (e. g. for Tanker, Disembarkation)	ⓘ Note
1.4			Pilots transferred by helicopter	ⓘ H
2			Pilot office with Pilot look-out. Pilot look-out	■ Pilot look-out
3	⊙ PIL STA	■ Pilots	Pilot office	■ Pilots
4			Port with Pilotage-Service	Port name (Pilots)

Coast Guard, Rescue Stations

10	✚ C G ⊙ R TR C G WALLIS SANDS	Coast Guard station	■ CG ⊚ CG ⌐CG
11		Coast Guard station with Rescue station	■ CG✚ ⊚ CG✚ ⌐CG✚
12	✚ ✚ LS S	Rescure station. Lifeboat station. Rocket station	✚
13		Lifeboat lying at a mooring	⛵✚ ✚
14		Refuge for shipwrecked mariners	Ref

Services

Signal Stations

			Signal station in general	⊚ SS		⚓ Sig Sta
0	⊙ SS		Signal station in general	⊚ SS		⚓ Sig Sta
1			Signal station, showing International Port Traffic Signals	⊚ SS (INT)		
2			Traffic signal station. Port entry and Departure signals	⊚ SS (Traffic)		
3	° HECP		Port control signal station	⊚ SS (Port control)		
4			Lock signal station	⊚ SS (Lock)		
.1			Bridge passage signal station	⊚ SS (Bridge)		
.2			Bridge lights including traffic signals	● F Traffic-Sig		
6			Distress signal station	⊚ SS		
7			Telegraph station	⊚ SS		
8	S Sig Sta		Storm signal station	⊚ SS (Storm)		
9	⊙ NWS SIG STA		National Weather Service signal station, Wind signal station	⊚ SS (Weather)		
0			Ice signal station	⊚ SS (Ice)		
1			Time signal station	⊚ SS (Time)		
.1		° Tide gauge	Tide scale or gauge	‡		
.2			Automatically recording tide gauge	⊚ Tide gauge		
3			Tidal signal station	⊚ SS (Tide)		
4			Tide stream signal	⊚ SS (Stream)		
5			Danger signal station	⊚ SS (Danger)		
6			Firing practice signal station	⊚ SS (Firing)		

Supplementary National Symbols

° BELL		Bell (on land)	
° MARINE POLICE		Marine police station	
° FIREBOAT STATION		Fireboat station	
🖵		Notice board	
⊙ LOOK TR		Lookout station; Watch tower ⌐	
Sem		Semaphore	
⬤		Park Ranger station	

U *Small Craft Facilities*

Small Craft Facilities

	Traffic Features, Bridges → D	Public Buildings, Cranes → F	Pilots, Coastguard, Rescue, Signal Stations →
1.1		Boat harbor, Marina	⚓
1.2		Yacht berths without facilities	
2		Visitors' berth	
3		Visitors' mooring	
4		Yacht club, Sailing club	
5		Slipway	
6		Boat hoist	
7		Public landing, Steps, Ladder	
8		Sailmaker	
9		Boatyad	
10		Public inn	
11		Restaurant	
12		Chandler	
13		Provisions	
14		Bank, Exchange office	
15		Physician, Doctor	
16		Pharmacy, Chemist	
17		Water tap	
18		Fuel station (Petrol, Diesel)	
19		Electricity	

Small Craft Facilities

I0		Bottle gas
I1		Showers
I2		Laundrette
I3		Public toilets
I4		Post box
I5		Public telephone
I6		Refuse bin
I7		Car park
I8		Parking for boats and trailers
I9		Caravan site
I0	△	Camping site
I1		Water Police

Marina facilities

No	LOCATION	Approach feet (reported)	Alongside feet (reported)	Electricity (transients)	Ramp surfaced/natural	Repairs hull/motor/radio	Marine railway feet	Lift capacity tons	Moorings berths	Boat rental	Food/Lodging	Toilets/Showers/Laundry	Pump-out/Winter storage	Water/Ice	Groceries/Hardware	Bait/Tackle	Nautical chart sales	Diesel oil/Gasoline
1	LAS VEGAS BOAT	80	20			S	HM			M		F C	T P	WD	C	W I	GH	BT	G
2	LAKE MEAD MAR	80	15	B E		S	HM			M		FL	T P	WD	C	W I			DG
3	HEMENWAY HARBOR	80				S													
4	TEMPLE BAR HAR	80	15			SN				M	H	FLC	TSL P	WD	C	W I	GH	BT	G
5	ECHO BAY RESORT	35	35	BM		S	M			M	H	FLC	TSL P	WD	C	W I	GH	BT	G
6	OVERTON BEACH	100				S				M		F C	TSL	WD		W I	G	BT	G
7	CALLVILLE BAY M	100	40			S				M	H	F C	TS P	WD		W I	G	B	G

(-) DENOTES HOURS LATER   (-) DENOTES HOURS EARLIER
THE LOCATIONS OF THE ABOVE PUBLIC MARINE FACILITIES ARE SHOWN ON THE CHART BY LARGE PURPLE NUMBERS.
THE TABULATED "APPROACH - FEET (REPORTED)" IS THE DEPTH AVAILABLE FROM THE NEAREST NATURAL OR DREDGED CHANNEL TO THE FACILITY.
THE TABULATED "PUMPING STATION" IS DEFINED AS FACILITIES AVAILABLE FOR PUMPING OUT BOAT HOLDING TANKS.
(H) APPROACH DEPTH FLUCTUATES WITH LAKE LEVELS.

AERO, Aero	Aero light	P 60	crs	Course	J 32
AERO, RBn	Aeronautical radiobeacon	S 16	Cup, Cup.	Cupola	E 10.4
Aero RC	Aeronautical radiobeacon	S 16	Cus Ho	Customs house	F 61
Al	Alternating	P 10.11	Cy	Clay	J 3
ALP	Articulated Loading Platform	L 12			
Alt	Alternating	P 10.11	D	Destroyed	0 94
Am	Amber	P 11.8	Destr	Destroyed	0 94
anc	Ancient	0 84	dev	Deviation	B 67
ANCH, Anch	Anchorage	N 20,	DIA, Dio	Diaphone	R 11
		0 21	Dir	Direction	P 30, P 3
approx	Approximate	0 90	dist	Distant	0 85
Apprs	Approaches	0 22	dm	Decimeter(s)	B 42
			Dn.	Dolphin	F 20
B	Boy, bayou	0 4	Dol	Dolphin	F 20
Bdy Mon	Boundary monument	B 24	DW	Deep Water route	M 27.1,
bk	Broken	J 33	12.4		
Bkw	Breakwater	F 4.1	DZ	Danger Zone	Q 50
Bl	Blue	P 11.4			
BM	Bench mark	B 23	E	East, eastern	B 10
Bn	Beacon	0 4	ED	Existence doubtful	I 1
Bn Tr	Beacon tower	0 3	EEZ	Exclusive Economic Zone	N 47
Br	Breakers	K 17	E Int	Equal interval, isophase	P 10.3
brg	Bearing	B 62	Entr	Entrance	0 16
brk	Broken	J 33	Est	Estuary	0 17
Bu	Blue	P 11.4	exper	Experimental	0 93
			Explos	Explosive	R 10
c	Course	J 32	Exting, exting	Extinguished	P 55
C	Con, cylindrical	Q 21			
C	Cove	0 9	f	Fine	J 30
CALM	Centenary Anchor Leg Mooring	L 16	F	Fixed	P 10.1
Cas	Castle	E 34.2	Fd	Fjord	0 5
Cb	Cobbles	J 8	F Fl	Fixed and flashing	P 10.10
cbl	Cable	B 46	FISH	Fishing	N 21
cd	Candela	B 54	Fl	Flashing	P 10.4
CD	Chart datum	H 1	Fla	Flare stack	L 11
Cem	Cemetery	E 19	fm	Fathom	B 48
CG	Coast Guard station	T 10	fms	Fathoms	B 48
Chan	Channel	D 14	fne	Fine	J 30
Ch.	Church	E 10.1	Fog Det Lt	Fog detector light	P 62
Chy	Chimney	E 22	Fog Sig	Fog signal	R 1
Cl	Clay	J 3	FP	Flagpole	E 27
CL	Clearance	D 20, D 21	FS, FS.	Flagstaff	E 27
cm	Centimeter(s)	B 43	ft	Foot, feet	B 47
Co	Coral	J 10			
Co rf	Coral reef	0 26	G	Gravel	J 6
Cr	Creek	0 7	G	Green	P 11.3

INDEX OF ABBREVIATIONS

	Gulf	O 3
*Fl	Group flashing	P 10.4
Occ	Group occulting	P 10.2
	Hard	J 39
	Hour	B 49
	Pilot transferred by helicopter	T 1.4
	Highest astronomical tide	H 3
Mr	Harbormaster	F 60
oric Wk	Historic wreck	N 26
	Horizontally disposed	P 15
Cl	Horizontal clearance	D 21
p	Hospital	F 62.2
	Hour	B 49
	Hard	J 39
	International Association of	Q 130
	Lighthouse Authorities	
	Inlet	O 10
ns	Intensified	P 45
Qk Fl	Interrupted quick flashing	P 10.6
	Interrupted quick flashing	P 10.6
Fl	Interrupted quick flashing	P 10.6
	Isophase	P 10.3
	Interrupted ultra quick	P 10.8
	Kilometer(s)	B 40
	Knot(s)	B 52
	Loch, lough, lake	O 6
	Lagoon	O 8
BY	Large Automatic Navigational Buoy	P 8
lat	Latitude	B 1
H	Lighter aboard ship	G 184
	Lowest astronomical tide	H 2
	Landing	F 17
	Leading	P 21
	Ledge	O 28
	Long flashing	P 10.5
	Landing	F 17
	Liquified natural gas	G 185
, long	Longitude	B 2
	Line of position	S 21, S 31,
	Liquified petroleum gas	G 186
	Life saving station	T 12

Lt	Light	P 1
Lt Ho	Lighthouse	P 1
LT V	Light vessel	O 6
m	Meter(s)	B 41
m	Minute(s) of time	B 50
m	Medium (in relation to sand)	J 31
M	Mud, muddy	J 2
M	Nautical mile(s)	B 45
mag	Magnetic	B 61
MHHW	Mean higher high water	H 13
MHLW	Mean higher low water	H 4
MHW	Mean high water	H 5
MHWN	Mean high water neaps	H 11
MHWS	Mean high water springs	H 9
Mi	Nautical mile(s)	B 45
min	Minute of time	B 50
Mk	Mark	Q 101
MLHW	Mean lower high water	H 15
MLLW	Mean lower low water	H 12
MLW	Mean low water	H 4
MLWN	Mean low water neaps	H 10
MLWS	Mean low water springs	H 8
mm	Millimeter(s)	B 44
Mo	Morse	P 10.9
MON, Mon	Monument	B 24, E 24
MSL	Mean sea level	H 6
Mt	Mountain	O 32
Mth	Mouth	O 19
N	North, northern	B 9
N	Nun	Q 20
NE	Northeast	B 13
NM	Nautical mile(s)	B 45
N Mi	Nautical mile(s)	B 45
No	Number	N 12.2
Np	Neap tide	H 17
NW	Northwest	B 15
NWS SIG STA	Weather signal station	T 29
Obsc	Obscured	P 43
Obscd	Obscured	P 43
Obs spot	Observation spot	B 21
Obstn	Obstruction	K 40, K 41,
		K 42
Obstr	Obstruction	K 41

Oc	Occulting	P 10.2
Occ	Occulting	P 10.2
Occas	Occasional	P 50
ODAS	Ocean Data Acquisition System	Q 58
Or	Orange	P 11.7
P	Pebbles	J 7
P	Pillar	Q 23
PA	Position approximate	B 7
Pass	Passage, pass	O 13
PD	Position doubtful	B 8
P LT STA	Pilot station	T 3
Pk	Peak	O 35
Post Off	Post office	F 63
Priv, priv	Private	P 65, Q 70
Prod. Well	Production well	L 20
PROHIB	Prohibited	N 2.2, N 20, N 21
Pyl	Pylon	D 26
Q	Quick flashing	P 10.6
Qk Fl	Quick flashing	P 10.6
R	Coast radio station providing QTG services	S 15
R	Red	P 11.2
R	Rocky	J 9
Ra	Radar reference line	M 32
Ra (conspic)	Radar conspicuous object	S 5
Ra Antenna	Dish aerial	E 31
Racon	Radar transponder beacon	S 3
Radar Sc.	Radar scanner	E 30.3
Radar Tr.	Radar tower	E 30.2
Radome, Ra Dome	Radar dome	E 30.4
Ra Ref	Radar reflector	S 4
RBn	Circular radiobeacon	S 10
RC	Circular radiobeacon	S 10
Rd	Roads, roadstead	O 22
RD	Directional radiobeacon	S 11
RDF	Radio direction finding station	S 14
Rk	Rock	J 9
Rky	Rocky	J 9
R Mast	Radio mast	E 28
Ro Ro	Roll on Roll off	F 50
R Sta	Coast radio station providing QTG services	S 15

R Tower	Radio tower	E 29
Ru	Ruins	D 8, F 33
RW	Rotating radiobeacon	S 12
S	Sand	J 1
S	South, southern	B 11
S	Spar, spindle	Q 24
s	Second of time	B 51
SALM	Single Anchor Leg Mooring	L 12
SBM	Single Buoy Mooring	L 16
Sc	Scanner	E 30.3
Sd	Sound	O 12
SD	Sounding doubtful	I 2
SE	Southeast	B 14
sec	Second of time	B 51
sf	Stiff	J 36
sft	Soft	J 35
Sh	Shells	J 12
Shl	Shoal	O 25
Si	Silt	J 4
so	Soft	J 35
Sp	Spring tide	H 16
SP	Spherical	Q 22
Sp.	Spire	E 10.3
Spipe	Standpipe	E 21
SPM	Single point mooring	L 12
SS	Signal station	T 20
st	Stones	J 5
stf	Stiff	J 36
stk	Sticky	J 34
Str	Strait	O 11
Subm	Submerged	O 93
Subm piles	Submerged piles	K 43.1
sy	Sticky	J 34
SW	Southwest	B 16
T	True	B 63
t	Metric ton(s)	B 53
Tel	Telephone, telegraph	D 27
Temp, temp	Temporary	P 54
Tk	Tank	E 32
Tr, Tr., TR	Tower	E 10.2, 20
TT	Tree tops	C 14
TV Mast	Television mast	E 28
TV Tower	Television tower	E 29

INDEX OF ABBREVIATIONS

V   INDEX OF ABBREVIATIONS

Supplementary National Abbreviations

Apt	Apartment	Es		HWF & C	High water full and change	Hh
				Hz	Hertz	Bg
B	Black	Qq				
bk	Black	Jas		in	Inch	Bc
bl	Black	Jas		ins	Inches	Bc
Blds	Boulders	Je		Inst	Institute	En
br	Brown	Jaz		ISLW	Indian springs low water	Hg
bu	Blue	Jau				
				K	Kelp	Ju
Cap	Capitol	Et		kc	Kilocycle	Bk
Ch	Chocolate	Jba		kHz	Kilohertz	Bh
Chec	Checkered	Qo		kn	Knot(s)	Ho
Ck	Chalk	Jf				
Cn	Cinders	Jp		La	Lava	Jl
Co	Company	Eu		LLW	Lower low water	He
Co Hd	Coral head	Ji		LOOK TR	Lookout tower	Tf
COLREGS	Collision regulations	Na		lrg	Large	Jai
Corp	Corporation	Ev		lt	Light	Jbc
cps	Cycles per second	Bj		Ltd	Limitd	Er
CRD	Columbia River Datum	Hj		LW	Low water	Hc
c/s	Cycles per second	Bj		LWD	Low water datum	Hd
Ct Ho	Court house	Eo		LWF & C	Low water full and change	Hi
dec	Decayed	Jan		m2	Square meter(s)	Ba
deg	Degree(s)	Bn		m3	Cubic meter(s)	Bb
Di	Diatoms	Jaa		Ma	Mattes	Jag
Diag	Diagonal bands	Qp		Magz	Magazine	El
Discol water	Discoloured water	Ke		Mc	Megacycle(s)	Bl
dk	Dark	Jbd		Mds	Madrepores	Jj
				MHz	Megahertz	Bi
Explos Anch	Explosives anchorage	Qk		Mn	Manganese	Jq
				Mo	Morse code	Rf
Facty	Factory	Ed		Ms	Mussels	Js
F Gp Fl	Fixed and group flashing	Pd		MTL	Mean Tide Level	Hf
fl	Flood	Hq				
fly	Filnty	Jao		NAUTO	Nautophone	Rc
Fr	Foraminifera	Jy				
Fu	Fucus	Jaf		or	Orange	Jax
				Oys	Oysters	Jr
GAB, Gab	Gable	Ei		Oz	Ooze	Jb
GCLWD	Gulf Coast Low Water Datum	Hk				
Gl	Globigerina	Jz		Pav	Pavillion	Ep
glac	Glacial	Jap		Pm	Pumice	Jm
gn	Green	Jav		Po	Polyzoa	Jad
Govt Ho	Government house	Em		Pt	Pteropods	Jac
Grd	Ground	Ja				
Grs	Grass	Jv		Quar	Quarantine	Fd
gty	Gritty	Jam		Qz	Quartz	Jg
GUN	Fog gun	Rd				
gy	Gray	Jbb		Rd	Radiolaria	Jab
				rd	Red	Jay
HECP	Harbor entrance control point	Tb		rt	Rotten	Jaj
HHW	Higher high water	Hb		Ry	Railway, Railroad	Db
HS	High school	Eg				
ht	Height	Hp		Sc	Scoriae	Jo
HW	High water	Hq		Sch	Schist	Jh

INDEX OF ABBREVIATIONS

Supplementary National Abbreviations

ɔ	School	Ef
ɔn	Semaphore	Tg
	Shingle	Jd
Fl	Short-long flashing	Pb
ʷ	Small	Jah
ɹ	Sponge	Jt
	Spicules	Jx
ɩ	Speckled	Jal
⸱	Seatangle	Jw
M	Statute mile(s)	Be
Mi	Statute mile(s)	Be
	Stream	Hl
	Streaky	Jak
B-BELL	Submarine fog bell	Ra
ɔm crib	Submerged crib	Ki
B-OSC	Submarine oscillator	Rb
ɔ vol	Submarine volcano	Kd
	Telephone	Eq, Qt
	Short ton(s)	Bm
	Tufa	Jn
	Telegraph	Qs
off	Telegraph office	Ek
⸱	Tenacious	Jaq
ɘv	Uneven	Jbf
v	University	Eh
	Microsecond(s)	Bf
⸱c	Microsecond(s)	Bf
ɽ	Varied	Jbe
	Velocity	Hn
	Violet	Jat
Ash	Volcanic ash	Jk
	White	Jar
IS	Whistle	Qc
	Yard	Bd
⸱	Yards	Bd
	Yellow	Jaw

W International Abbreviations

B Positions, Distances, Directions, Compass

PA	Position approximate	B 7
PD	Position doubtful	B 8
N	North	B 9
E	East	B 10
S	South	B 11
W	West	B 12
NE	Northeast	B 13
SE	Southeast	B 14
NW	Northwest	B 15
SW	Southwest	B 16
km	Kilometer(s)	B 40
m	Meter(s)	B 41
dm	Decimeter(s)	B 42
cm	Centimeter(s)	B 43
mm	Millimeter(s)	B 44
M	Nautical mile(s), Sea mile(s)	B 45
ft	Foot/feet	B 47
h	Hour	B 49
m, min	Minute(s) of time	B 50
s, sec	Second(s) of time	B 51
kn	Knot(s)	B 52
t	Ton(s)	B 53
cd	Candela (new candela)	B 54

D Cultural Features

Ru	Ruin	D 8

F Ports

Lndg	Landing for boats	F 17
RoRo	Roll-on, Roll-off Ferry	F 50

I Depths

ED	Existence doubtful	I 1
SD	Sounding doubtful	I 2

K Rocks, Wrecks, Obstructions

Br	Breakers	K 17
Wk	Wreck	K 20
Obstn	Obstruction	K 40

L Offshore Installations, Submarine Cables, Submarine Pipeline

Fla	Flare stack	L 11
Prod	Submerged Production	L 20
Well	Well	

M Tracks, Routes

Ra	Radar	M 31
DW	Deep Water	M 27.2

N Areas, Limits

No	Number	N 12.2
DW	Deep Water	N 12.4

O Hydrographic Terms

Smt	Seamount	O 33

Lights

Light	P 1
Fixed	P 10.1
Occulting	P 10.2
Isophase	P 10.3
Flashing	P 10.4
Long-flashing	P 10.5
Quick	P 10.6
Interrupted quick	P 10.6
Very quick	P 10.7
Interrupted very quick	P 10.7
Ultra quick	P 10.8
Interrupted ultra quick	P 10.8
Morse Code	P 10.9
white	P 11.1
red	P 11.2
green	P 11.3
blue	P 11.4
violet	P 11.5
yellow/orange/Amber	P 11.6
orange	P 11.7
Amber	P 11.8
Leading light	P 20.3
Direction light	P 30
occasional	P 50
Air obstruction lights	P 61.2
Fog detector light	P 62
Aeronautical	P 60/61.1

Buoys, Beacons

Black	Q 81
Mark	Q 101
International Association of Lighthouse Authorities	

Fog Signals

Explosive	R 10
Diaphone	R 11
Whistle	R 15

S — Radar, Radio, Electronic Position-Fixing Systems

Ra	Coast Radar Station	S 1
Racon	Radar transponder beacon	S 3
RC	Circular (non-directional) marine radiobeacon	S 10
RD	Directional radiobeacon	S 11
RW	Rotating-pattern radiobeacon	S 12
RG	Radio direction-finding stations	S 14
R	QTG service, Coast radio stations	S 15
Aero RC	Aeronautical radiobeacon	S 16
WGS	World Geodetic System	S 50

T — Services

H	Pilots transferred by helicopter	T 1.4
SS	Signal station	T 20
INT	international	T 21

IALA MARITIME BUOYAGE SYSTEM
LATERAL MARKS REGION A

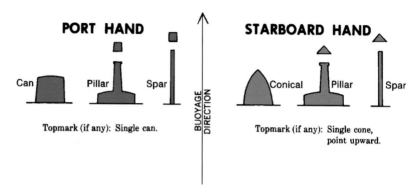

PORT HAND

Can   Pillar   Spar

BUOYAGE DIRECTION

Topmark (if any): Single can.

STARBOARD HAND

Conical   Pillar   Spar

Topmark (if any): Single cone,
point upward.

Lights, when fitted, may have any phase
characteristic other than that used
for preferred channels.

Examples

Quick Flashing
Flashing
Long Flashing
Group Flashing

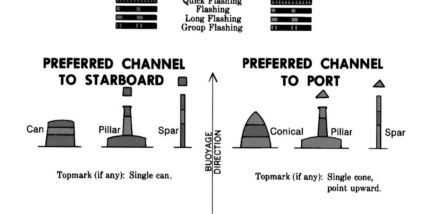

PREFERRED CHANNEL
TO STARBOARD

Can   Pillar   Spar

BUOYAGE DIRECTION

Topmark (if any): Single can.

PREFERRED CHANNEL
TO PORT

Conical   Pillar   Spar

Topmark (if any): Single cone,
point upward.

Lights, when fitted, are composite
group flashing Fl (2 + 1).

IALA MARITIME BUOYAGE SYSTEM
LATERAL MARKS REGION B

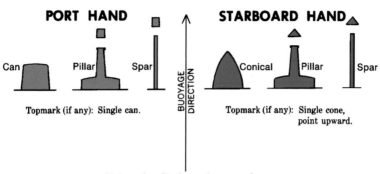

PORT HAND

Can   Pillar   Spar

Topmark (if any): Single can.

BUOYAGE DIRECTION

STARBOARD HAND

Conical   Pillar   Spar

Topmark (if any): Single cone, point upward.

Lights, when fitted, may have any phase
characteristic other than that used
for preferred channels.

Examples
Quick Flashing
Flashing
Long Flashing
Group Flashing

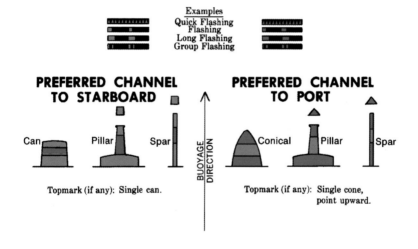

**PREFERRED CHANNEL
TO STARBOARD**

Can   Pillar   Spar

Topmark (if any): Single can.

BUOYAGE DIRECTION

**PREFERRED CHANNEL
TO PORT**

Conical   Pillar   Spar

Topmark (if any): Single cone, point upward.

Lights, when fitted, are composite
group flashing Fl (2+1).

IALA MARITIME BUOYAGE SYSTEM
CARDINAL MARKS REGIONS A AND B

Topmarks are always fitted (when practicable).
Buoy shapes are pillar or spar.

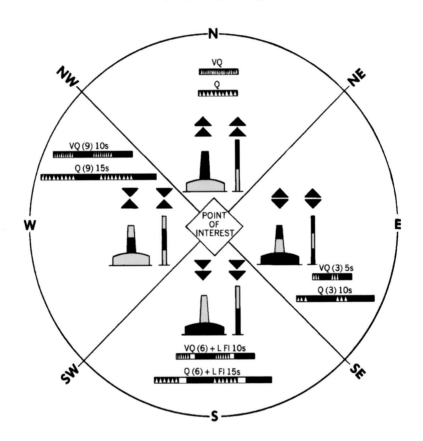

Lights, when fitted, are **white** , Very Quick Flashing
or Quick Flashing; a South mark also has a
Long Flash immediately following the quick flashes.

IALA MARITIME BUOYAGE SYSTEM
REGIONS A AND B

ISOLATED DANGER MARKS

Topmarks are
always fitted
(when practicable).

Light, when fitted, is
white
Group Flashing (2)

Fl (2)

Shape: Optional, but not
conflicting with lateral
marks; pillar or spar
preferred.

SAFE WATER MARKS

Topmark (if any):
Single sphere.

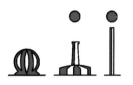

Light, when fitted,
is **white**
Isophase or Occulting,
or one Long Flash
every 10 seconds or
Morse "A"

Iso

Occ

L Fl 10s

Morse "A"

Shape: Spherical
or
pillar or spar.

SPECIAL MARKS

Topmark (if any):
Single X shape.

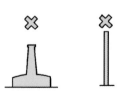

Light (when fitted) is
yellow and may have
any phase characteristic
not used for white lights.

Examples
Fl Y
Fl (4) Y

Shape: Optional, but not
conflicting with
navigational marks.

III

Aids to Navigation

A

TYPES OF AIDS

Unlike the roads and highways that we drive on, the waterways we go boating on do not have road signs that tell us our location, the route or distance to a destination, or of hazards along the way. Instead, the waterways have aids to navigation—all those man-made objects used by mariners to determine position or a safe course. These aids also assist mariners in making landfalls, mark isolated dangers, enable pilots to follow channels, and provide a continuous chain of charted marks for precise piloting in coastal waters. An aid to navigation system is designed, and intended, to be used with a nautical chart. The exact meaning of an aid may not be clear to a navigator unless the appropriate chart is consulted, because the chart illustrates the relationship of the individual aid to channel limits, obstructions, hazards to navigation, and to the total aid-to-navigation system.

The term *aid to navigation* (the U.S. Coast Guard uses the acronym ATON) includes buoys, daybeacons, lights, lightships, radio beacons, and sound signals. (The United States no longer has any lightships or marine radio beacons, but these may be found in some foreign waters.). Also included are the Global Positioning System (GPS), Loran, and other electronic systems. The term aid to navigation covers all the visible, audible, and electronic signals that are established by government and private authorities for piloting purposes.

The term *aid to navigation* encompasses a wide range of floating and fixed objects ("fixed" means attached to the bottom or shore), ranging from a small buoy or a single pile of wood, concrete, or metal with a sign, to lighthouses with an array of visible, audible, and electronic signals. Informal aids, such as bush stakes marking natural channels or hazards in a creek, are not a part of the organized system of aids to navigation.

Prominent buildings, cupolas, smokestacks, and other structures ashore as well as unique land features, also can be used as signposts for navigation. These are LANDMARKS, as distinguished from aids established solely for navigation.

MAJOR TYPES

BUOYS are floating objects—other than lightships—that are anchored to the bottom as aids to navigation. They have distinctive shapes and colors, as determined by location and purpose, and may emit visible, audible, and/or electronic signals.

BEACONS are aids to navigation that are permanently fixed to the earth's surface, on shore or in the water; they may be of any size, from a lighthouse to a single pile. Lighted beacons are called LIGHTS; unlighted beacons are called DAYBEACONS.

Beacons are equipped with one or more DAYMARKS of a distinctive shape and color for daytime identification. Lights are classified by the U.S. Coast Guard and other authorities as PRIMARY SEACOAST LIGHTS, SECONDARY LIGHTS, or MINOR LIGHTS, as determined by their location, importance, and physical characteristics. A light's range and intensity vary according to its classification. The shape and color of its supporting structure may be distinctive to identify it, but these characteristics do not convey information as they do for buoys. The term LIGHTHOUSE is often applied to primary seacoast lights and to some secondary lights; see **Figure III-1**.

SOUND SIGNALS are activated to assist mariners during periods of low visibility. They may occasionally be separate aids, as when located on the end of a jetty, but are generally part of a buoy, light, or larger aid to navigation.

RANGES are pairs of unlighted or lighted fixed aids that, when observed in a line, show the pilot to be on the centerline of a channel. Individual structures may also serve to mark a turn in a channel.

LIGHTSHIPS are specially equipped vessels anchored at specific locations to serve as aids to navigation. They are of distinctive shape and color, and have lights, sound signals, and radio beacons. In U.S. waters, lightships have been replaced by permanent towers

Figure III-1 *Buoys, daybeacons, and minor lights all follow a systematic pattern of shapes and colors, whereas primary lights, such as lighthouses, are more distinctive and diverse.*

and large, specially equipped buoys, as explained later in this chapter.

RADIO BEACONS are transmitters broadcasting a characteristic signal specifically to aid navigation at night, in fog, or at distances exceeding normal visibility. These are usually located at another aid, such as a major light, but may be separate.

RADIONAVIGATION SYSTEMS are radio transmitters ashore and on satellites that emit special signals for use in navigation in fog or when beyond sight of land or offshore aids. The systems include Loran-C and the Differential Global Positioning System (DGPS) operated by the Coast Guard; the Global Positioning System (GPS) operated by the Department of Defense; and aeronautical radio beacons and Omni stations run by the Federal Aviation Administration. There are also some private systems, but these are seldom be available to recreational boaters.

B

BUOYS

Buoys are anchored to the sea bottom at specific locations, and are shown on charts by special symbols and lettering that indicate their shape, color, and visual and/or sound signals (if any). They vary widely in size. Buoys are secured to the sea bottom, using chain, to heavy concrete "sinkers" weighing up to six tons or more. The length of the chain will vary with the location, but may be as much as three times the depth of the water.

The buoyage system adopted for U.S. waters consists of several different types of buoys, each designed to serve under definite conditions. Broadly speaking, all buoys serve as daytime aids; in addition, many have lights and/or sound signals so that they may be used at night and in periods of poor visibility.

A buoy's shape, color, and light characteristics, if any, give a navigator information about his location and the safe guidance of his vessel. A buoy's size is usually determined by the importance of the waterway and size of the vessels using it, as well as the distance at which the buoy must be seen.

BUOY CHARACTERISTICS

Buoys may be unlighted or lighted, sound buoys, or combination buoys (emitting both an audible and a visual signal). The Coast Guard maintains about 20,000 unlighted and 4,100 lighted and combination buoys in waters under its jurisdiction. Additional buoys are maintained by state and private agencies in nonfederal waters.

Buoy Shapes

Unlighted buoys may be further classified by their shape.

CAN BUOYS have a cylindrica,l above-water appearance, like a can or drum floating with its axis vertical and flat end upward; see **Figure III-2**. Two lifting lugs may project slightly above the flat top of a can buoy, but they do not significantly alter its appearance.

Figure III-2 *A can buoy is cylindrical in shape with a long vertical axis. On some buoys, the upper part is made of metal plates at right angles to each other, making an excellent radar reflector. Most, but not all, can buoys are constructed in this manner.*

NUN BUOYS have an above-water appearance like that of a cylinder topped with a cone, pointed end up; see **Figure III-3**. The cone may come to a point or be slightly rounded. Smaller nun buoys have a single lifting ring at the top; larger buoys have several lugs around the sides.

Unlighted buoys come in standard sizes; a nun's above-water portion may vary from 30 inches (0.76 m) to 14 feet (4.27 m); can buoys range from roughly 18 inches (0.46 m) to nearly 10 feet (3.05 m) above the waterline. Boaters should remember that a considerable portion of a buoy is underwater, so that it is actually much larger and heavier than would appear from casual observation. Some smaller, temporary buoys are now made of plastic materials.

Figure III-3 *A nun buoy is cylindrical up to just above the waterline; from there it tapers to form a conical top. This small nun buoy has a lifting ring at its top; this has no navigational significance. The upper part of some nun buoys consists of metal plates at right angles to reflect radar signals.*

SPHERICAL BUOYS are now used in the revised U.S. lateral system for a specific purpose as discussed later.

Other buoys of special shapes will sometimes be found in use as markers, but these are not regular aids to navigation. The Coast Guard has now eliminated the use of SPAR BUOYS, but they may be used in some other nations or in private systems. They are usually large vertical logs, trimmed, shaped, and appropriately painted; they are anchored at one end by a chain.

Lighted, sound, and combination buoys are described by their visual and/or audible signals rather than by their shape, as discussed in the following section; see **Figure III-4**.

Sound Buoys

A separate category of unlighted buoys includes those with a characteristic sound signal to aid in their location in fog or other conditions of reduced visibility. Different sound signals are used to distinguish between different buoys that are within audible range of each other.

BELL BUOYS are steel floats surmounted by short skeleton towers in which a bell is mounted; see **Figure III-5**. They are effective day and night, and especially in fog or other conditions of

Figure III-4 *Buoys with lights or sound signals, or both, have no significant shape, although most will appear similar to the one shown at right. Lifting lugs are at the base of the superstructure.*

Figure III-5 *A bell buoy has four tappers that are outside the bell. These strike the bell, making similar sounds in an irregular pattern as the buoy rocks with the motion of the sea.*

reduced visibility; their use is favored because of their moderate maintenance requirements. Bell buoys are operated by motion of the sea using four tappers, loosely hung *externally* around the bell. When the buoy rolls in waves, wakes, or groundswells, a single note is heard at irregular intervals. Bell buoys, and other types that require some sea motion to operate, are not normally used in sheltered waters; a horn buoy is used there instead if a fog signal is needed.

GONG BUOYS are similar in construction to bell buoys, except they have multiple gongs instead of a single bell. They normally have four gongs of different tones with one tapper for each gong. As the sea rocks the buoy, the tappers strike against their gongs, sounding four different notes in an irregular sequence.

WHISTLE BUOYS have a whistle sounded by compressed air that is produced by sea motion. Whistle buoys are thus used principally in open and exposed locations where a groundswell normally exists.

HORN BUOYS are rather infrequently used. They differ from whistle buoys in that they are electrically powered; they are placed where a sound signal is needed and where sea motion cannot be depended upon.

Lighted Buoys

Buoys may be equipped with lights of various colors, intensities, and flashing characteristics (called RHYTHMS). Colors and characteristics of the light convey specific information to the mariner. Intensity depends upon the distance at which the aid must be detected, as influenced by such factors as background lighting and normal atmospheric clarity.

Lighted buoys are metal floats with a battery-powered light atop a short skeleton tower; see **Figure III-6**. Lighted buoys can operate for many months without servicing and have "daylight controls" that automatically turn the light on and off as darkness falls and lifts. The lights are powered by storage batteries that are kept charged by panels of solar cells near the top of the buoy.

Lights on buoys may be red, green, white, or yellow according to the specific function of the buoy.

Figure III-6 *A lighted buoy has a light at its top that flashes in one of several regular patterns. The light is turned off in daylight by a photoelectric sensor. Power is obtained from a battery that is kept charged by a solar panel.*

Combination Buoys

Buoys with both a light and a sound signal are designated COMBI-NATION BUOYS. Typical of these are "lighted bell buoys," "lighted gong buoys," and "lighted whistle buoys." There will be only one type of sound signal on any buoy; see **Figure III-7**.

Figure III-7 *This combination buoy has both a light and a whistle as a sound signal. The whistle is operated by air that is compressed by the motion of the buoy.*

Offshore Buoys

As a replacement for lightships, and for use at important offshore locations, the U.S. Coast Guard had developed LARGE NAVIGATIONAL BUOYS (LNBs) These aids—sometimes referred to as "superbuoys"—had combined a light and a sound signal, and often also had a radio beacon. This type of buoy had been roughly 40 feet (12.2 m) in diameter with a superstructure rising to 30 feet (9.1 m) or more.

Because of their high initial cost and considerably greater maintenance costs, LNBs have been replaced with EXPOSED LOCATION BUOYS (ELBs). Although not of the size of LNBs, these are still quite large, being 9 feet (2.74 m) in diameter. ELBs are equipped with lights and sound signals, as well as weather and electronic navigation devices. Power is supplied by batteries kept charged by solar cells and a generator powered by wave motion; see **Figure III-8**.

Figure III-8 *Exposed location buoys (ELBs) are usually equipped with a racon (radar beacon), light, and sound signal; some will have meteorological sensors. These typically have both solar and wave-actuated power sources.*

Color of Buoys

Buoys may be of one solid color, or have a combination of two colors in *horizontal bands* or *vertical stripes*. The colors used in the IALA system are red, green, yellow, white, and black.

Optical Reflectors

Almost all unlighted buoys are fitted with areas of reflective material, to help boaters find them at night by using searchlights. The material may be red, green, white, or yellow in banding or patches, and it has the same significance as lights of these colors. It can also be placed on the numbers or letter of lighted and unlighted buoys of all types.

Radar Reflectors

Many buoys have RADAR REFLECTORS—vertical metal plates set at right angles to each other so as to greatly increase the echo returned to a radar receiver on a vessel. The plates are shaped and mounted to preserve the overall characteristic shape of an unlighted buoy or the general appearance of a lighted buoy; refer to **Figure III-2**.

LIGHT RHYTHMS

The lights on lighted buoys will generally flash in one of several specific rhythms, for these reasons:

- Flashing conserves the energy source within the buoy.
- A flashing light can be more easily detected against a background of other lights.
- The light can signal specific information during hours of darkness, such as the need for special caution at a certain point in a channel.
- Different flashing patterns can be used to distinguish clearly among buoys of similar functions that are within visible range of each other.

FLASHING lights are those that come on for a single brief flash at regular intervals; the time of light is always *less* than the time of darkness. Coast Guard–maintained flashing buoys will flash their light not more than 30 times per minute; this is the more generally used characteristic. It is sometimes referred to as "slow flashing," though this is not an official designation.

QUICK FLASHING lights will flash not less than 60 times each minute. These buoys are used for special situations where they can be more quickly spotted and where particular attention to piloting is required.

GROUP FLASHING (2+1) lights show two brief flashes, a brief interval of darkness, a single brief flash, and then an interval of darkness of several seconds' duration.

MORSE CODE (A) flashing lights have a cycle of a short flash,

CAUTIONS IN USING BUOYS

Do not count on floating aids always maintaining their precise charted positions or unerringly displaying their characteristics. The Coast Guard works constantly to keep aids on station and functioning properly, but obstacles to perfect performance are so great that complete reliability is impossible.

Buoys are heavily anchored, but may shift, be carried away, or sunk by storms or ships. Heavy storms may also cause shoals to shift relative to their buoys.

Lighted buoys may malfunction and show no light, or show improper light characteristics. Audible signals on most buoys are operated by action of the sea, and may be silent in calm water; or they may fail to sound because of a broken mechanism.

A buoy does not maintain its position directly over its sinker, as it must have some scope of movement on its anchor chain. Under the influences of current and wind, it swings in small circles around the sinker, which is anchored at the charted location. This swinging is unpredictable, and a boat attempting to pass too close risks colliding with a yawing buoy. In extremely strong current, a buoy may even be pulled beneath the water surface.

Buoys may be temporarily removed for dredging operations, and/or in northern waters, they may be discontinued for the winter, or changed to special types in order to prevent damage or loss from ice floes. The *Light Lists* show dates for changes or for seasonal buoys, but these are only approximate and may be changed by weather or other conditions.

Temporary or permanent changes in buoys may be made between editions of charts. Keep informed of existing conditions through reading *Notices to Mariners* and/or *Local Notices to Mariners*.

All buoys (especially those in exposed position) should therefore be regarded as warnings or guides, and *not as infallible navigation marks*. Whenever possible, navigate with bearings or angles on fixed aids or objects on shore, and by soundings, rather than by total reliance on buoys.

and a brief dark interval, then a longer flash and a longer dark interval, repeated every eight seconds. This is the "dot-dash" of the letter "A" in Morse code.

The above light rhythms are shown diagrammatically in **Figure III-9**. The PERIOD of a light is the time it takes to complete one full cycle of flash and dark interval, or flashes and dark, intervals. A light described as "Flashing 4 seconds" has a period of four seconds. One flash and one dark interval lasts just that long before the cycle is repeated. Three standard periods are used for flashing lights: intervals of 2.5, 4, and 6 seconds.

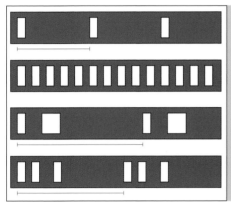

Figure III-9 *Characteristic light patterns identify buoys. They are named (as indicated in these schematic patterns) and identified on charts by abbreviations. One period is indicated by* ⊢————————————⊣ *(quick flashing is continuous and does not have a period).*

The term CHARACTERISTICS, as applied to a lighted aid to navigation, includes the color as well as the rhythm, and may also cover physical features, such as nominal range.

C

DAYBEACONS

Daybeacons are unlighted aids that are fixed, rather than floating like buoys. They may be either on shore or in waters up to about 15 feet (4.6 m) deep.

Daybeacons vary greatly in design and construction, depending upon their location and the distance from which they must be seen. Daybeacons in U.S. waters, and their chart symbols, are illustrated in the ATON *Light List* plates.

DAYBEACON CONSTRUCTION

The simplest daybeacon is a single pile with signboards, called *dayboards*, at or near its top, usually two, facing in opposite directions; see **Figure III-10**. The pile may be wood, concrete, or metal.

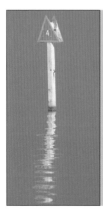

Figure III-10 *Most daybeacons consist of a single pile with two dayboards. At some locations, such as channel junctions, where the daybeacon can be approached from more than two directions, there will be an additional dayboard. Some daybeacons consist of multiple pile structures; these have no navigational significance.*

A larger, more visible, and more sturdy daybeacon is the "three-pile dolphin" type: three piles a few feet apart at their lower ends, bound tightly together with wire cable at their tops. There are also some five-pile dolphins (four piles around one central pile.) The Coast Guard maintains approximately 10,000 daybeacons.

Dayboards

To serve its purpose on an aid to navigation, a dayboard usually bears identification in the form of a number or, occasionally, a letter or a number plus a letter.

Dayboards are normally either square or triangular, corresponding to can and nun buoys, respectively. Square dayboards are green with green reflective border. Triangular dayboards are red with red reflective border. The number or letters will also be of reflective material. In special applications, a dayboard may be octagonal (eight-sided) or diamond-shaped, carrying a brief warning or notice.

THE USES OF DAYBEACONS

For obvious reasons, the use of daybeacons is restricted to relatively shallow waters. Within this limitation, however, they are often more desirable than buoys because they are firmly fixed in position and taller, and thus easier to see and identify. Daybeacons also require less maintenance than buoys.

Daybeacons are used primarily for channel marking, and they serve in the same manner as buoys in the buoyage systems to be described later in this chapter.

D

MINOR LIGHTS

J ust as daybeacons are sometimes substituted for unlighted buoys, so, too, may lighted buoys be replaced with MINOR LIGHTS. These are fixed structures of the same overall physical features as daybeacons, but equipped with a light generally similar in characteristics to those found on buoys; see **Figure III-11**. Most minor lights are part of a series marking a channel, river, or harbor; also included, however, are some isolated single lights if they are of the same general size and characteristics. The term "minor light" does not include the more important lights marking harbors, peninsulas, major shoals, etc. These have lights of greater intensity and/or special characteristics; these are designated as "secondary" or "primary sea-coast" lights and are discussed in detail later in this chapter.

Figure III-11 *Most minor lights are little more than a day-beacon to which has been added a light, with its battery box and solar panels. The minor light seen here has a more elaborate structure and has three dayboards.*

FEATURES OF MINOR LIGHTS

Minor lights are placed on a single pile, on multiple-pile dolphins, or on other structures in the water, or on shore; see **Figure III-12**. Minor lights carry dayboards for identification, and reflective material for nighttime safety should the light be extinguished.

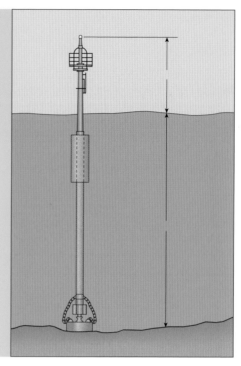

Figure III-12 *An articulated light is a rigid, buoyant structure fixed (with an articulated coupling) to the seabed. It provides a more precise location than an anchored, lighted buoy. Without the light, it would be an articulated daybeacon.*

LIGHT CHARACTERISTICS

A minor light normally has the same color and flashes with the same phase characteristics as a lighted buoy; refer to **Figure III-9**. Intensity will generally approximate that of a lighted buoy, but visibility may be increased by its greater height above water and its more stable platform. A combination of storage batteries and solar cells is used in the same manner as on lighted buoys.

Sound Signals

Minor lights may, in some locations, emit an audible signal—an electrically operated horn or siren. In some cases, the signal operates continuously for months when reduced visibility conditions can be expected.

BUOYAGE SYSTEMS

Most maritime nations use either a LATERAL SYSTEM OF BUOYAGE or a CARDINAL SYSTEM, or both. In the lateral system, the buoys indicate the direction to a danger relative to the course that should be followed. In the cardinal system, characteristics of buoys indicate the location of the danger relative to the buoy itself; see **Figure III-13**. The term "cardinal" relates to cardinal points of the compass.

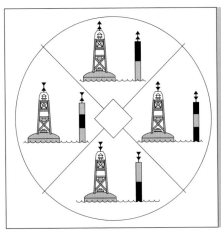

Figure III-13 *Cardinal marks, named for the four points of the compass, indicate that the navigable water lies to the named side of the mark. If lighted, the color is white.*

THE IALA SYSTEMS OF AIDS TO NAVIGATION

The International Association of Marine Aids to Navigation and Lighthouse Authorities (formerly the International Association of Lighthouse Authorities, still known as the IALA) had the goal of establishing a single global system of aids to navigation, but was unable to do so and had to settle for two regional systems. These systems have many identical characteristics, but also one fundamental difference—the colors used for the lateral marks. Both systems have provisions for the use of topmarks: small shapes, such as spheres and triangles, placed above the basic buoy structure.

The IALA-A System

The IALA-A system uses the same cardinal marks, isolated danger marks, safe water marks, and special marks as the IALA-B system. The difference is that the lateral marks are directly opposite in color—marks; left to starboard when entering from the sea are colored green, those on the port side are colored red. The shapes of the lateral marks are the same in both systems, only the color is different.

The IALA-A system is used in all waters worldwide that are not covered by the IALA-B system. IALA-A, of course, includes European, African, and nearly all Asian waters.

The IALA-B System

The full name is "System B—The Combined Cardinal and Lateral System (Red to Starboard)." System B uses five types of "marks"—those of lateral and cardinal systems, plus three different marks for isolated dangers and safe waters, and for special indications. These are all of a designated design, but may vary in size. Nations using this system must use aids conforming to the basic designs, but need not use all types. As indicated by the title, lateral marks on the starboard side of channels entering from the open sea are colored red, with the port side being marked by green aids. **Table III-1** summarizes the IALA-B System.

The IALA-B system is used in the Western Hemisphere, *including the United States and Canada*, Japan, Korea, and the Philippines.

THE U.S. AIDS TO NAVIGATION SYSTEM

The United States has long used a lateral system of buoyage; this has now been converted to conform, as noted above, to the colors

IALA-B LATERAL SYSTEM OF BUOYAGE

| Returning from sea* | Color | Number | Unlighted Buoy Shape | Lights or Lighted Buoys | | Daymark Shape |
				Light Color	Light Rhythm	
To your starborad	Red	Even	Nun	Red	Flashing or quick flashing	Triangular
To your portside	Green	Odd	Can	Green	Flashing or quick flashing	Square
Preferred channel	Red-and-green horizontally banded**	Not numbered; may be lettered	Nun or can **	Red or green	Group flashing (2 + 1)	Triangular or square **
Midchannel of fairway	Red-and-white, white vertically striped	Not numbered; may be lettered	Spherical or sound buoy	White	Morse code "A" flashing	Octagonal

* or entering a harbor from a larger body of water, such as a lake.
** preferred channel is indicated by color of uppermost band, shape of unlighted buoy, and color of light, if any.

Table III-1 *This table summarizes the color numbering, shape, and lights or buoys used in the IALA-B system of buoyage. Be aware of the "clockwise direction" rule in the coastal waters of the United States (see text).*

and shapes established by the IALA for "System B." Wherever you travel in the navigable waters of the United States, Canada, and other countries of the Western Hemisphere, the basic system is the same; you needn't learn a new system for new waters. (The IALA-A system is used in U.S. possessions west of the International Date Line and south of 10° North latitude.)

In the United States, the lateral system of buoyage is uniformly used in all federal jurisdiction areas and on many other bodies of water where it can be applied. In this system, the shape, coloring, numbering, and light characteristics of buoys are determined by their position with respect to the navigable channel, natural or dredged, as such channels are entered and followed *from sea* toward the head of navigation. This is termed the "Conventional Direction of Buoyage."

Because not all channels lead or appear to lead from seaward, certain arbitrary assumptions are used in order that the lateral system may be consistently applied. In coloring and numbering offshore buoys along the coasts, the following system has been adopted: proceeding in a southerly direction along the Atlantic Coast, in a northerly then westerly direction along the Gulf Coast, and in a northerly direction along the Pacific Coast will be considered the same as coming in from seaward. This can be remembered as proceeding around the coastline of the United States in a *clockwise* direction.

Thus, there's a very important exception to red-right and green-left. As noted above, it occurs in the United States when a channel that appears to come from the sea has in fact been designated by the U.S. Coast Guard as part of the "clockwise direction" rule. It happens in coastal waters, including rivers, and especially in the Intracoastal Waterway. Many unexpected groundings have occurred because the navigator did not study the charts or did not understand the clockwise rule.

On the Great Lakes, offshore buoys are colored and numbered as proceeding from the outlet end of each lake toward its upper end. This will be generally westerly and northward on most Great Lakes, except on Lake Michigan, where it will be southward. Buoys marking channels into harbors are colored and numbered just as for channels leading into coastal ports from seaward.

On the Mississippi and Ohio rivers and their tributaries, characteristics of aids to navigation are determined as proceeding from seaward toward the head of navigation. However, local terminology describes "left bank" and "right bank" as proceeding *with* the flow of the river.

Not all types of marks are used in all waters, but those that are used will conform to the IALA-B system with respect to shapes, colors, topmarks, and light color and rhythm (characteristic). The U.S. system does not use cardinal buoys, but does use safewater buoys and a few isolated danger buoys. The IALA-B system makes no mention of sound signals such as gongs or whistles on buoys, and the previous U.S. usage has not been changed. The U.S. system also includes daybeacons and lights on fixed structures—aids that are not covered by either IALA system.

The U.S. system of lateral aids to navigation is supplemented by nonlateral aids where appropriate; see **Figure III-14**.

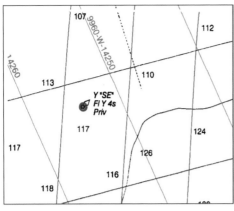

Figure III-14 *There are some circumstances in the IALA-B system where yellow buoys that have no lateral significance are used. Generally, these mark anchorages, exclusion areas, etc.*

Coloring

All buoys are painted distinctive colors to indicate on which side you should pass them, or to show their special purpose. In the lateral system, the significance of colors is as described below; the traditional phrase "red, right, returning" helps in remembering the system.

Red buoys mark the starboard ("right") side of a channel when entering ("returning") from seaward, or a hazard that you must pass by, keeping the buoy to starboard.

Green buoys mark the port (left) side of a channel when entering from seaward, or an obstruction that must be passed by keeping the buoy on the left side.

Red-and-green horizontally banded buoys are used to mark the "preferred" channel (usually the major channel) at junctions, or hazards that you may pass on *either* side (but check your chart to be sure). If the topmost band is green, the preferred channel is with the buoy to port—it is treated as if it were a can buoy. If the topmost band is red, the preferred channel is with the buoy to starboard. (Note: When proceeding *toward* the sea, it may *not* be possible to pass such buoys safely on either side. This is particularly true in situations where you are following one channel downstream, and another channel joins in from the side; see **Figure III-15**. When such a buoy is spotted, be sure to consult the chart for the area.)

Red-and-white vertically striped buoys are "safewater marks"; they are used as offshore approach points (often called "sea buoys"), and to mark a fairway or midchannel. If lighted, there will be a red

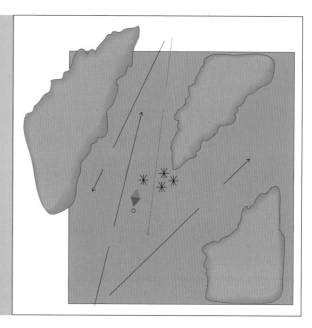

Figure III-15 *A junction buoy, painted with red and green bands, must be treated differently depending upon whether you are proceeding toward the sea or away from it. Upstream, either course is safe; downstream one course is dangerous.*

spherical TOPMARK above the light that is roughly one-fifth the diameter of the buoy. If unlighted, these may be spherical or they may be similar in construction to sound buoys and will have a topmark.

Red-and-black horizontally banded buoys are used to mark obstructions; the top band will be black.

Note carefully that areas of color running horizontally are "bands"; if the areas are arranged vertically, they are "stripes." These terms are used in other color combinations in the case of special-purpose buoys.

Shapes of Buoys

In the lateral system of buoyage, unlighted buoys have definite shape characteristics that indicate which side of the channel they mark. The ability to distinguish shapes is particularly essential when you first sight a buoy in line with the sun and can see only its silhouette, rather than its color.

Can buoys, painted green, mark either the port (left) side of the channel when returning from seaward or a hazard that you must pass by keeping the buoy to port.

Nun buoys, painted red, mark the starboard (right) side of channels, or hazards that must be passed by keeping the buoy to starboard.

Channel junction may be of either can or nun shape, as determined by which is the primary channel. If the buoy is a *can*, the uppermost band is *green*; if the buoy is a *nun*, the uppermost band is *red*; refer to **Figure III-15**. Obstruction buoys follow the same color scheme.

Unlighted red-and-white vertically striped buoys are spherical in shape with a topmark.

No special significance is to be attached to the shape of sound, lighted, or combination buoys. The purpose of these is indicated by their coloring, number, or the rhythm of the light. Special caution must be exercised when a buoy is first sighted under conditions that its color cannot be determined, such as when proceeding in a direction toward which the sun is low in the sky.

Numbering

Most buoys have "numbers" that actually may be numbers, letters, or a number-letter combination to help you find and identify them on charts. In the lateral system, numbers serve as yet another indication of which side the buoy should be passed. The system is as follows:

Odd-numbered buoys mark the port (left) side of a channel leading in from seaward. In accordance with the rules stated above, these will be green buoys, or cans if they are unlighted.

Even-numbered buoys mark the starboard (right) side of a channel; these will be red (nun) buoys.

Numbers increase from seaward and are kept in approximate sequence on the two sides of a channel by omitting numbers as appropriate if buoys are not uniformly placed in pairs. Occasionally, numbers will be omitted on longer stretches without buoys, to allow for possible later additions. Numbers followed by letters, such as "24A" and "24B," are buoys added to a channel after the initial numbering system was established, and with the series not yet renumbered.

A buoy marking a wreck will often carry a number derived from the number of the buoy next downstream from it, preceded by the letters "WR." Thus, a buoy marking a wreck on a channel's left-hand side between buoys 17 and 19 would be "WR17A." A wreck buoy not related to a channel may be designated by one or two letters, relating to the name of the wrecked vessel or a geographic location.

Letters without numbers are sometimes used for red-and-white vertically striped buoys marking fairways or harbor entrances, and for green-and-red horizontally banded buoys.

Numbers followed by letters may be used on aids to navigation marking offshore dangers. For a buoy marked "1JR," the number has the usual sequential significance, and the letters "JR" indicate that it is off "Johnson Reef."

Color of Lights

For all lighted buoys in the IALA-B lateral system, the following system of colors is used:

Green lights on buoys mark the left-hand side of a channel returning from seaward; these are on green odd-numbered buoys, or green-and-red horizontally banded buoys with the green band uppermost.

Red lights on buoys mark either the right-hand side of a channel when entering from sea (red even-numbered buoys) or red-and-green horizontally banded buoys with the red band uppermost.

White lights in the IALA-B system are used only on safewater marks with the Morse letter "A" rhythm, and on marks at isolated dangers with a group flashing (2) rhythm. (Some white lights remain in use on the Western Rivers—the Mississippi River and its tributaries above Baton Rouge, Louisiana, and on some other rivers that flow toward the Gulf of Mexico—but will eventually be eliminated.)

Yellow lights are used only on special marks; their rhythm may vary, but usually is flashing or fixed.

Light Rhythms

Flashing lights are placed only on green or red buoys, or on special-purpose buoys.

Quick flashing lights are placed only on channel-edge-marking green and red buoys; these are used to indicate that special caution in piloting is required, as at sharp turns or changes in the width of the waterway, or to mark hazards that must be passed only on one side.

Group flashing (2 + 1) lights are used only on buoys with red-and-green horizontal bands. These are the buoys at channel junctions and at obstructions that can be passed on either side.

Morse code "A" flashing lights are placed only on red-and-white vertically striped buoys that mark a fairway or midchannel; these are passed closely on either side and are always white.

Fixed lights show continuously; they are rarely used because of excessive power requirement compared with the various types of flashing lights.

Daybeacons and Minor Lights

The lateral system of buoyage has been described in terms of unlighted and lighted buoys, but the descriptions also apply fully to comparable daybeacons and minor lights.

Daybeacons with red triangular dayboards may be substituted for nun buoys, or ones with green square dayboards may replace can buoys. Minor lights may be used in place of lighted or combination buoys. Structures subject to being repeatedly struck by vessels may be set back from the channel edge, as noted in the *Light List*.

If a daybeacon is used to indicate the preferred channel at a junction, or at an obstruction, the dayboard will be red-and-green horizontally banded, with the color of the uppermost band indicating the main or preferred channel. The dayboard shape will be either square or triangular, as determined by the color or the top band, as with a can or nun buoy used for this purpose.

Safewater daybeacons marking fairways or the midchannel have an octagonal-shaped dayboard, painted red and white, and divided in half vertically down the middle.

A diamond-shaped dayboard has no significance in the lateral system. A typical application might be to increase the daytime detectability of a minor light that is not a part of a channel or waterway series. These are often used to mark a shoal, rock, submerged object, or other hazard; they are also used to mark prohibited areas where boats must not enter.

Minor lights, and the lights on buoys, are equipped with electronic DAYLIGHT CONTROLS that automatically turn the light on during periods of darkness and off during daylight. These controls are not of equal sensitivity; therefore, all lights do not go on and off at the same time. Take care to identify aids correctly during twilight periods when some may be on but others may not.

Wreck Buoys

Buoys that mark dangerous wrecks are generally lighted and placed on the seaward or channel side of the obstruction, as near to it as possible. Wreck buoys are solid red or green if they can be safely passed on only one side, horizontally banded otherwise, and numbered as previously discussed. Be careful around wreck buoys, because sea action may have shifted the wreck since the last Coast Guard visit. Wreck buoys are also used in some instances where a fixed aid to navigation has been knocked down but the remains have not been removed.

Isolated Danger Marks

In addition to the widespread lateral system of buoyage, the U.S. Coast Guard maintains a few aids to navigation in the cardinal system of buoyage. Such an aid is erected on, or moored above or near, an "isolated danger" that has unobstructed water on all sides. These marks should not be approached closely without special caution. Colors are red and black, horizontally banded; if lighted, the light is always white and group flashing (2), at 6-second. A topmark of two black spheres, vertically arranged, is used on lighted and unlighted buoys; no numbers are used, but they may be lettered.

Seasonal Buoys

In some areas subject to severe icing during winters, the normal buoys are removed to prevent damage or loss. These are temporarily replaced with ice buoys: lighted or unlighted buoys of special sturdy construction. The placement and removal of such buoys are announced in *Local Notices to Mariners* and *Light List* changes. In some instances, lights on shore may be activated to guide vessels in the absence of buoys.

Racons

Some major aids to navigation are equipped with RADAR BEACONS, commonly shortened to RACONS. When a racon is triggered by pulses from a vessel's radar, it transmits a reply that results in a better defined display on that vessel's radarscope, thus increasing accuracy of range and bearing measurements.

The reply may be coded to facilitate identification, in which case it will consist of a series of dots and dashes: short and/or long intensifications of the radar blips beginning at and extending beyond the racon's position on the radar screen. The range is the measurement on the radarscope to the dash nearest its center. If the racon is not coded, the beacon's signal will appear as a radial line extending from just beyond the reflected echo of the aid, or from just beyond where the echo would be seen if detected. Details of racon coding will be found in the *Light Lists*. The coded response of a racon may not be received if the radar set is adjusted to remove interference (IF) or sea return from the scope; interference controls should be turned off when reception of a racon signal is desired.

SPECIAL-PURPOSE AIDS

The Coast Guard also maintains several types of special-purpose aids, with no lateral significance, to mark anchorages, fishnet areas, dredging limits, etc.

In the IALA-B system of buoyage, these are all yellow, regardless of the usage to which they are being put. These may be of can or nun shape, and, if lighted, the light will be yellow with any rhythm (fixed or slow flashing preferred). (Some are equipped with xenon-discharge-tube lights that give a very bright, but very brief, flash.) Dayboards on a daybeacon or minor light will be diamond shaped and all yellow in color.

REPORTING DISCREPANCIES

All boaters should realize that the U.S. Coast Guard cannot keep the many thousands of aids to navigation under constant observation. For that reason, it is impossible to maintain every light, buoy, daybeacon, and fog signal operating properly and on its charted position at all times. The safety of all who use the waters will be enhanced if every person who discovers an aid missing, off station, or operating improperly will notify the nearest Coast Guard unit of the situation that has been observed. Use radio, land telephone, Internet e-mail, or postal mail, as dictated by the urgency of the report.

VARIATIONS IN THE BASIC U.S. SYSTEM

Although all U.S. waters are marked by the basic U.S. Aids to Navigation system, there are some areas in which additional or modified markings are used to meet local needs.

Buoyage on the Western Rivers

Buoyage on the "Western Rivers"differs from the basic U.S. system in several ways:

- Aids to navigation are not numbered.
- Any numbers on aids to navigation are of no lateral significance, but show (statute) mileage from a fixed point—usually the river mouth.
- Diamond-shaped crossing dayboards, red and white or green and white as appropriate, are used to indicate where the river channel crosses from one bank to the other.
- Lights on green aids to navigation show a single-flash characteristic, which may be green or white.
- Lights on red aids to navigation show a group (2) flashing characteristic, which may be red or white.
- Isolated danger and safewater marks are not used.

In an effort to eliminate white light from the lateral buoyage system, the U.S. Coast Guard is attempting to restrict this color's use to only crossing daymarks.

Intracoastal Waterway Aids to Navigation

The Intracoastal Waterway (ICW) runs parallel to the Atlantic and Gulf coasts from Norfolk, Virginia, to the Mexican border. The purpose of the ICW is to provide a protected route for vessels making coastwise passages. Distances along the ICW are in statute miles because the waterway is maintained by the U.S. Army Corps of Engineers.

Distinctive ICW markings. Aids to navigation on the ICW are conventional buoys, daybeacons, and minor lights, but with added identification of yellow triangles on "red" aids and yellow squares on "green" aids; see **Figure III-16**.

Figure III-16 *The dayboards on day-beacons and minor lights on the Intracoastal Waterway carry the usual numbers but also a yellow triangle or square. Buoys also have such a mark toward the sea or away from it. Upstream, either course is safe; downstream, one course is dangerous.*

The conventional direction of buoyage in the ICW is generally southerly along the Atlantic coast, and first northerly then westerly along the Gulf of Mexico coast. Intracoastal Waterway aids are numbered in groups—usually not exceeding "99," beginning again with "1" or "2" at specified natural dividing points.

Buoy lights follow the standard system of red lights on red buoys and green lights on green buoys. Colors of minor lights fit the same pattern. Range lights, not being a part of the lateral system, may be of any standard color.

Dual-purpose aids. The ICW was stitched together out of local rivers, channels, and fairways (with some additional land cuts created), which are marked in the conventional manner of the basic U.S. system. Some aids to navigation on these local waterways may also serve the Intracoastal Waterway. If they have this DUAL PURPOSE, some portion of them is identified with either a yellow square (indicating a can buoy) or a yellow triangle (indicating a nun buoy). In some cases, a green can buoy marking a local channel may carry a yellow triangle for the ICW.

No matter what its basic shape, any aid carrying a yellow triangle should be left to starboard when following the ICW from north to south and on the Gulf Coast. Similarly, any aid with a yellow square should be left to port. Where dual markings are employed, the ICW skipper should disregard the basic shape and coloring of the aid on which the yellow square or triangle is placed, and pilot his craft *solely* by the shape of the yellow markings. The numbers on the aids will be those of the local channel's lateral system, and in some instances where the southward ICW proceeds down a river, the numbers will temporarily decrease rather than increase.

Nonlateral aids in the ICW—such as safewater marks, isolated danger marks, and ranges—will have a horizontal band or bar in yellow.

Uniform State Waterway Marking System

Each state has authority over control of navigation on waters that lie wholly within its boundaries and that are not subject to federal jurisdiction. This includes the responsibility for establishing and maintaining aids to navigation. In 1966, the UNIFORM STATE WATERWAY MARKING SYSTEM (USWMS) was developed for these waters to indicate safe boating channels and areas by marking the presence of either natural or artificial hazards. With trailer-borne boats traveling freely over the highways from state to state, the gain for recreational boaters from the uniform system is obvious.

A major defect in the USWMS, however, was its evident contradictions with the U.S. Aids to Navigation system that is based on IALA-B. The U.S. Coast Guard initiated a plan in 1998 to replace aids of the USWMS with aids consistent with the system used in coastal waters. The USWMS will have been completely superceded by December 31, 2003.

Inland Waters Obstruction Mark. To meet the needs of boaters on inland waters after the demise of the USWMS, one new aid to navigation was created. On inland navigable waters designated by the Commandant of the Coast Guard as "State waters," and on nonnavigable waters of a state where there is no defined head of navigation, such as lakes, the INLAND WATERS OBSTRUCTION MARK will be used to indicate that an obstruction extends from the nearest shore out to that buoy. This buoy will have black-and-white vertical stripes, and its meaning will be "Do not pass between this buoy and the shore." If lighted, it will have a quick-flashing white characteristic. It replaces the red-and-white vertically striped buoy of the USWMS, whose color had a different, and contradictory, meaning in the basic coastal system.

INFORMATION AND REGULATORY MARKERS

Although not derived from the IALA-B system, the U.S. Aids to Navigation system includes INFORMATION AND REGULATORY MARKS (often called "markers"). These are used to alert skippers to various warning or regulatory matters. They may be either buoys or beacons.

These marks have orange geometric shapes against a white background. The meanings associated with the orange shapes are as follows:

- An open-faced diamond signifies danger.
- A vertical diamond shape with a cross centered within it indicates that vessels are excluded from the marked area.
- A circular shape indicates that certain operating restrictions are in effect within the marked area.
- A square or rectangular shape contains directions or instructions lettered within the shape.

When a buoy is used as an information or regulatory mark, it must be white in color with two horizontal orange bands placed completely around the buoy circumference. One band must be near the top of the buoy body, and the other just above the waterline; both bands must be clearly visible.

OTHER BUOYAGE SYSTEMS

In Canadian waters, the lateral system of buoyage is essentially the same as in the United States. Minor differences in the physical appearance of buoys may be noted, but these are not great enough to cause confusion. Cardinal buoys of the IALA-B system are used in some areas; boaters there should familiarize themselves with the appearance and meaning of such aids. Chart symbols, likewise, may be slightly different from those standardized for use on the U.S. charts.

Skipper's Responsibility

Familiarize yourself with the system of buoyage that you expect to encounter before entering coastal waters of another nation. Consult the appropriate official publications or cruising guides for the necessary information.

PRIMARY SEACOAST AND SECONDARY LIGHTS

RIMARY SEACOAST AND SECONDARY LIGHTS in the United States are so designated because of their greater importance as aids to navigation. They differ from minor lights previously considered by their greater physical size, intensity of light, and complexity of light characteristics. These lights are more diverse than minor lights and buoys; only broad, general statements can be made about them as a group.

Primary seacoast lights warn the high-seas navigator of the proximity of land. They are the first aids seen when making a landfall (except where there may be a light tower). A coastwise navigator can use these lights to keep farther offshore at night than would be possible by using other visual aids. These are the most powerful and distinctive lights in the U.S. Aids to Navigation system.

Primary seacoast lights may be located on the mainland or offshore, on islands and shoals. Offshore, they may mark a specific hazard or they may serve merely as a marker for ships approaching a major harbor.

Many primary seacoast lights are classified according to the importance of their location, the intensity of their light, and the prominence of their structure. Other aids are classed as secondary lights because of their lesser qualities in one or more of these characteristics. The dividing line is not clear, however, and lights that seem to fall more properly in one category may be classified in the other group in the *Light Lists*. The difference in classification is of no real significance to boaters and can be ignored in practical piloting situations.

STRUCTURES

The physical structure of a primary seacoast light and of many secondary lights is generally termed a LIGHTHOUSE, although this is not a designation used in the *Light Lists*. The structure's principal purpose is to support a light source and lens at a considerable height above water. The same structure may also house a sound signal or other equipment, and quarters for the operating personnel. Auxiliary equipment and personnel are sometimes housed instead in a group of buildings nearby in which case the whole group is referred to as a LIGHT STATION.

Lighthouses vary greatly in their outward appearances, depending on where they are, whether they are in the water or on shore, the light's importance, the ground they stand on, and the prevalence of violent storms; see Figures **III-17**, **III-18**, and **III-19**.

Lighthouse structures also vary according to the range of visibility they need: a lengthy range requires a tall tower or a high point of land, with a light of high CANDLEPOWER—the standard measure of brightness. At points intermediate to principal lights, however, and where ship traffic is light, long range is not so necessary, and a simpler structure can be used.

Coloring of Structures

Lighthouses or other light structures are marked with colors, bands, stripes, and other patterns to make them stand out against their backgrounds, and to assist in their identification; see **Figure III-20**.

LIGHT CHARACTERISTICS

Primary seacoast and secondary lights have distinctive light characteristics—lights of different colors, and lights that show continuously while others show in patterns. Their three standard colors are white, red, and green.

Figure III-17 *New London Ledge Light, Connecticut.*

Figure 5-18 *Split Rock Lighthouse State Park, Lake Superior, Minnesota.*

Figure III-19 *Kilauea Point Lighthouse, Kauai, Hawaii.*

Figure III-20 *Bands of stripes of various colors are often used to aid in distinguishing lighthouses from their backgrounds, and as a aid to identification.*

Light Rhythms

Varying the intervals of light and darkness in both simple and complex ways yields many different rhythms for major lights.

Fixed. A light is termed "fixed" if it is always on with no periods of darkness.

Flashing. The term "flashing" has already been defined as a light that is on less than it is off, in a regular sequence of single flashes occurring less than 30 times each minute. Some primary seacoast and secondary lights will "flash" in accordance with this definition, although their characteristics will have no relation to the flashes of buoys and minor lights. In general, a flashing major light will have a longer period (time of one complete cycle of the characteristic) and may have a longer flash—for example, the Cape Hatteras Light flashes once every 15 seconds with a 3-second flash.

In most instances, however, the actual light source is constant, and the "flashes" are produced by a rotating set of optical lenses; at close ranges, a weak, steady light may be seen. Although a few major lights have a "fixed" characteristic (a continuous light without change of intensity or color), the light-phase characteristics of primary seacoast or secondary lights are generally more complex, as described below (with current abbreviations); see **Table III-2**.

Group Flashing (Fl [n]) The cycle of the light characteristic consists of two or more flashes separated by brief intervals and followed by a longer interval of darkness. (The "n" in the abbreviation indicates the number of flashes.)

Alternating Flashing (Al Fl) Flashes of alternating color, usually white and red, or white and green.

Occulting (Oc) The light is on more than it is off; the interval of time that the light is *lighted* is greater than the time that it is ECLIPSED—its period of darkness.

Isophase (Iso) Intervals of light and darkness are equal; the light is described in the *Light List* or on charts in terms of the period, the lighted and eclipsed portions each being half of that time. This was formerly known as an "equal interval light."

Group Occulting (Oc [n]) Intervals of light regularly broken by a series of two or more eclipses. This characteristic may have all eclipses of equal length, or one greater than the others. (The "n" in the abbreviation indicates the number of eclipses.)

CHARACTERISTICS OF LIGHTS

Flashing pattern & period ⊢─⊣	Type	Description	Abbreviation
	Fixed	A light showing continuously and steadily.	F
	Fixed and flashing	A light in which a fixed light is combined with a flashing light of higher luminous intensity.	F Fl
	Flashing	A flashing light in which a flash is regularly repeated (frequency not exceeding 30 flashes per minute).	Fl
	Group flashing	A flashing light in which a group of flashes, specified in number, is regularly repeated.	Fl (2)
	Composite group	A light similar to a group flashing light, except that successive groups in the period have different numbers of flashes.	Fl (2+1)
	Isophase	A light in which all durations of light and darkness are equal.	Iso
	Single occulting	An occulting light in which an eclipse, of shorter duration than the light, is regularly repeated.	Oc
	Group occulting	An occulting light in which a group of eclipses, specified in number, is regularly repeated.	Oc (2)
	Composite group	A light, similar to a group-occulting light, except that successive groups in a occulting have different numbers of eclipses.	Oc (2+1)
	Quick	A quick light in which a flash is regularly repeated at a rate of 60 per minute.	Q
	Interrupted quick	A quick light in which the sequence of flashes is interrupted by regularly repeated eclipses of constant and long duration.	IQ
	Group quick	A group of 2 or more quick flashes, specified in number, which are regularly repeated. (Not used in the waters of the United States.)	Q(3)
	Morse Code A	A light in which lights of two clearly different durations (dots and dashes) are grouped to represent a character or characters in Morse code.	Mo (A)
	Alternating	A light showing different colors alternately.	Al RW
	Long flashing	A flashing light in which the flash is 2 seconds or longer.	LFl

Complex Characteristics

The above light-phase characteristics may be combined. Examples might include Gay Head Light's "Alternating White/Red 15 seconds (Al W R 15s)," where there is a white flash for 0.2 seconds, an eclipse (period of darkness) for 7.3 seconds, a red flash for 0.2 seconds, and an eclipse of 7.3 seconds, for a total period of 15 seconds; or Minots Ledge Light's "Group Flashing White 45 seconds (Fl W (1+4+3) 45s)," where 1.5–second white flashes occur at 1.5–second intervals in groups of one, four, and three, separated by 5–second intervals and followed by a 15.5–second longer interval to indicate the proper starting point of the 45–second period; or other characteristics of a generally similar nature.

Sectors

Many lights will have SECTORS—portions of their all-around arc of visibility in which the normally white light is seen as red or green. These sectors mark shoals or other hazards, or warn of land nearby.

Lights so equipped show one color from most directions, but a different color or colors over definite arcs of the horizon as indicated on charts and in the *Light List*. A sector changes the color of a light when viewed from certain directions, but *not* the flashing or occulting characteristic. For example, a flashing white light with a red sector, when viewed from within the sector, will appear as flashing red; see **Figure III-21**, left.

Sectors may be a few degrees in width, as when marking a shoal or rock, or wide enough to extend from the direction of deep water to the shore. Bearings referring to sectors are expressed in degrees *as they are observed from a vessel toward the light.*

You should almost always avoid water areas covered by red sectors, but you should also check your chart to learn the extent of the hazard. Some lights are basically red (for danger) with one or more white sectors indicating the direction of safe passage, but a narrow white sector of another light may simply mark a turning point in a channel.

Lights may also have sectors in which the light is *obscured*—it cannot be seen. These will be shown graphically on charts (see **Figure III-21**, right) and described in the *Light Lists.*

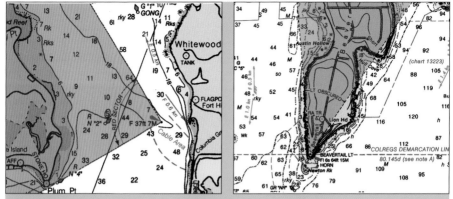

Figure III-21 *A hazardous area is often covered by a red sector of a light, and this sector (or sectors) is indicated by words along the arc on a chart (left). Aside from being red, the sector shows the same characteristics as the normal white sector of the light. A light may also be obscured over a sector, and this, too, is indicated on the chart. Note: The colors used here are for clarity and do not actually appear on a normal*

THE VISIBILITY OF LIGHTS

A light's theoretical visibility in clear weather depends on two factors: its intensity and its height above water. Its intensity fixes its NOMINAL RANGE, which is defined in the *Light Lists* as "the maximum distance at which the light may be seen in clear weather (meteorological visibility of 10 nautical miles)."

Height is important because of the earth's curvature; height determines the GEOGRAPHIC RANGE at which the light can be seen. It is not affected by the intensity (provided that the light is bright enough to be seen out to the full distance of the geographic range).

The nominal range of major lights is generally greater than the geographic range, and the distance from which such aids can be seen is limited only by the earth's curvature. Such lights are often termed "strong"; a light limited by its luminous range is a "weak light."

The glare, or LOOM, of strong lights is often seen far beyond the normal geographic range, and under rare atmospheric conditions the light itself may be visible at unusual distances. The range of visibility is obviously lessened by rain, fog, snow, haze, or smoke.

U.S. Coast Guard's *Light Lists* show the nominal range for all

CAUTIONS IN USING LIGHTS

Complex lights with several luminous ranges may appear differently at extreme distances where, for example, a white fixed (or flashing) light could be seen but a red flash of the same light was not yet within luminous range. Examination of a *Light List* will show that usually the nominal range of a red or green light is 15 percent to 30 percent less than that of the white light from the same aid. Be cautious when identifying lights like these.

The effect of fog, rain, snow, and haze on the visibility of lights is obvious. Colored lights are more quickly lost to sight in poor weather than are white lights. On the other hand, refraction may also cause a light to be visible from a greater distance than normal.

Be cautious also when using light sectors in your navigation. The actual boundaries between the colors are not so distinct as the chart suggests; the lights shade gradually from one color into the other.

Note, too, that the increasing use of brilliant shore lights for advertising, illuminating bridges, and other purposes may cause marine navigational lights, particularly those in densely populated areas, to be outshone and difficult to distinguish from the background lighting.

A light can also be extinguished for some reason. Unattended lights that are broken may not be immediately detected and corrected. If you do not see a light reasonably soon after your course and speed suggest that you should, check the situation carefully. Do not rely on any one light, except perhaps for making a landfall. For positive identification, use *several lights together* as a system, checking each against the others.

lighted aids except private aids, navigation ranges, and directional lights, and show how to convert nominal range to LUMINOUS RANGE—the maximum distance at which a light may be seen in specific *existing* visibilities. Both nominal and luminous ranges take no account of elevation, observer's height of eye, or the curvature of the earth. (Any height of eye on board the vessel increases the effective geographic range for that specific situation.) For lights of complex characteristics, nominal ranges are given for each color and/or intensity.

The geographic range of lights is not given in the *Light Lists* but can be determined from the given height of the light source. The distance to the horizon may be taken from a table in the front pages of each *Light List* volume, or calculated using the equation $D = 1.17 \sqrt{H}$ (where H is the height in feet and the distance is in nautical miles) or $D = 2.12 \sqrt{H}$ (where H is in meters and distance is still in nautical miles). For distances in statute miles, the factors are 1.35 and 2.44, respectively.

For any situation, the light's range, as limited by the earth's curvature, will be the distance to the horizon for the light *plus* the distance to the horizon for your height of eye—determine each distance separately, then add; *do not add heights and make a single calculation*. Boaters should know their height of eye when at the controls of their boat (and the height of any other position on board to which they can climb to see farther).

Lights on inland waters, where their radius of usefulness is not great, are frequently "weak" lights, whose intensity need not reach the full limit of their geographic range.

IDENTIFICATION OF LIGHTS

Charts can only briefly describe the characteristics of a primary seacoast or secondary light—by means of abbreviations and a notation of the total period of the light cycle. You will often need to consult the *Light Lists* for details of the characteristics to help you identify it positively.

When you first see a light, note its color, and time its full cycle of light changes. If color, period, and number of flashes per cycle match the *Light List* information, the light has been identified. As a precaution, however, check the charts and *Light Lists* to be sure that no other light in the vicinity has similar characteristics.

Emergency Lights

Emergency lights of reduced nominal range are displayed from many light stations when the main light is inoperative. These standby lights may or may not have the same characteristics as the main light. The existence of the standby light (if any) and its characteristics (if different) is noted in the *Light Lists*.

G

SOUND SIGNALS

A sound-producing instrument, operated in time of fog or other condition of reduced visibility from a definite point shown on a chart, serves as a useful sound signal. To use it effectively as an aid to navigation, you must be able to identify it and know its location.

As mentioned, the simpler sound signals used on buoys are operated by sea action, and thus you may have difficulty identifying them. Sound signals at all lighthouses and other lights are electronically or mechanically operated on definite time schedules, however, and so are easier to identify positively.

SIGNAL CHARACTERISTICS

Sound signal characteristics are described in terms of the length of a total cycle of one or more blasts of specific length and one or more SILENT INTERVALS, also of definite lengths. These times are shown in the *Light Lists* to aid in identification. (Normally, only the type of sound signal, without further details, is indicated on charts.) When you are counting the blasts and timing their cycle, refer to the *Light Lists* for details.

Sound Signal Equipment

Sound signals also differ from each other in tone, which helps in identification. The signal type for each station is shown in the *Light Lists* and on charts.

Diaphones produce sound by means of a slotted reciprocating piston activated by compressed air. Blasts may consist of two tones of different pitch, in which case the first part of the blast is higher pitched and the latter is lower. These alternately pitched signals are termed "two-tone."

CAUTIONS IN USING SOUND SIGNALS

Sound signals obviously depend upon the transmission of sound through the air. As aids to navigation, they thus have inherent limitations that you *must* consider. Because sound travels through air in a variable and unpredictable manner, you should note the following:

- The distance at which a sound signal can be heard may vary at any given instant according to the bearing of the signal, and may be different on different occasions.
- Under certain atmospheric conditions, you may hear only part of a sound signal that is a siren or that has a combination of high and low tones.
- There are sometimes areas close to a signal where you will not hear it, perhaps when the signal is screened by intervening landmasses or other obstructions, or when it is on a high cliff.
- The apparent loudness of a sound signal may be greater at a distance than in its immediate vicinity.
- A patch of fog or smoke may exist at a short distance from a manned station but not be seen from it. Thus the signal may not be placed in operation.
- Some sound signals require a start-up interval.
- You may not hear a sound signal with your boat's engine on, but you may hear it suddenly when it is off or if you go forward on board away from its noise.

In summary, sound signals are valuable as warnings, but do not place implicit reliance upon them in navigating your vessel.

Based on the above established facts, you must *NOT* assume:

- That you are out of the ordinary hearing distance of a sound signal because you do not hear it.

- That because you hear a sound signal faintly, you are at a distance from it.
- That you are near to the sound signal because you hear it clearly.
- That the sound signal is not sounding because you do not hear it, even when you know that you are nearby.
- That the detection distance and sound intensity under any one set of conditions is an infallible guide for any future occasion.

RANGES AND DIRECTIONAL LIGHTS

anges and directional lights serve to indicate the centerline of a channel and thus aid in the safe piloting of a vessel. Although they are used in connection with channels and other restricted waterways, and shown on all the appropriate charts, they are not a part of the lateral system of buoyage.

RANGES

A RANGE consists of two fixed aids to navigation so positioned with respect to each other that, when seen in line, they indicate that the observer's craft *may be in safe waters*; see **Figure III-23**. The aids may be lighted or unlighted, as determined by the importance of the range.

The conditional phrase "may be in safe waters" is used because observation of the two markers in line is *not* an absolute determination of safety. *A range is "safe" only within specific limits of distance from the front marker*. A vessel too close or too far away may be in a dangerous area. The aids that comprise the range do not in themselves indicate the usable portion of the range; check your chart and other aids.

Ranges are described in the *Light Lists* by first giving the position of the front marker, usually in terms of geographic coordinates—

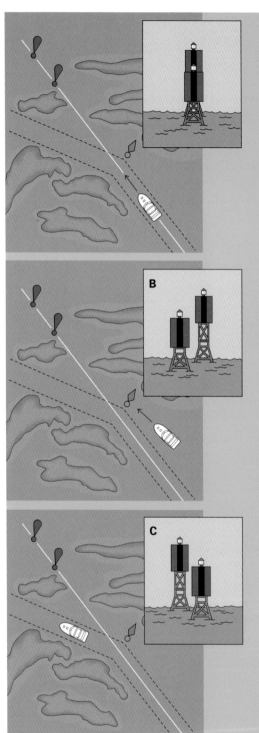

Figure III-22 *A skipper can keep within a narrow channel by following a range. At A, front and range markers are in line, with the higher rear range mark directly over the lower front mark. If he gets "off range," the markers will not be aligned, as shown in B. The channel may turn before reaching the range front marker, as in C; the turning point is normally marked by a buoy.*

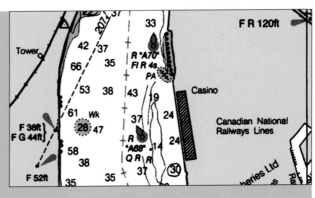

Figure III-23 *Lighted ranges are often used to mark channels in rivers, particularly where cross-currents exist. This range is on the St. Clair River on a true bearing of 207°. Range front light structures sometimes have all-around "passing lights" lower than the range light. The crossed-dashed line is the international border.*

latitude and longitude—and then stating the location of the rear marker in terms of direction and distance from the front marker. This direction, given in degrees and minutes, True, need not be used in ordinary navigation, but is useful in making checks of compass deviation. The rear dayboard (and light, if used) is always *higher* than the one on the front aid; see **Figure III-22**.

Because of their fixed nature, and the accuracy with which a vessel can be positioned by using them, ranges are among the best aids to navigation. Use a range whenever one is available; and use a buoy only to determine the beginning and end of the usable portion of the range.

Ranges are used outbound just as they are inbound. Make sure that you do not meet head-on with a vessel using the range in the opposite direction to your own.

Unlighted Ranges

Although any two objects may be used as a range, the term is properly applied only to those pairs of structures built specifically for that purpose. Special shapes and markings are used for the front and rear aids of a range for easier identification and more accurate alignment. Differing designs have been used in the past, but the Coast Guard has now standardized the use of rectangular dayboards, longer dimension vertical, painted in vertical stripes of contrasting colors. The design of specific-range dayboards will normally be found in the *Light Lists*.

Lighted Ranges

Because of their importance and high accuracy in piloting, most range markers are equipped with lights, in addition to the usual dayboards, to extend their usefulness through the hours of darkness. Entrance channels are frequently marked with range lights; the Delaware River on the Atlantic Coast and the Columbia River on the Pacific Coast are examples of this.

Range lights may be of any color used with aids to navigation—white, red, or green—and may show any of several characteristics. The principal requirement is that they be easily distinguished from shore backgrounds and from other lights. Front and rear lights will, however, normally be of the same color (white is frequently used because of its greater visibility range), with different rhythms. Since both lights must be observed together for the proper steering of the craft, range lights often have a greater "ON" interval than other lights do. Range rear lights are normally on for longer than their front counterparts; many ranges now show an isophase (equal interval) rear light and a quick-flashing front light.

Many range lights are fitted with special lenses that give a much greater intensity on the range centerline than off of it; the lights rapidly decrease in brilliance when observed from only a few degrees to either side. In some cases, the lights will be visible only from on or very near to the range line; in other cases, a separate, lower light of lesser intensity may be seen all around the horizon—this can be either from the main light source or from a small auxiliary "passing" light. Light is shown around the horizon when the front aid also serves to mark the side of a channel at a turn.

Most lighted ranges are lit only at night or during periods of reduced visibility that will actuate their daylight sensors; during daytime, these ranges are used by aligning the dayboards. A more recent development is the "day/night range" that has two lights each on front and rear towers at slightly different heights; these lights will have the same flashing characteristic, but often different arcs of visibility and ranges. In addition to the daytime light, these ranges still have their distinctive dayboards.

DIRECTIONAL LIGHTS

The establishment of a range requires suitable locations for two aids, separated adequately both horizontally and vertically. In some areas, this may not be possible, and a single light of special characteristics will be employed.

A DIRECTIONAL LIGHT is a single light source fitted with a special lens so as to show a white light in a narrow beam along a desired direction, with red and green showing to either side. The width of the sectors will depend upon the local situation, but red will be seen if the pilot is to the right of the centerline as he approaches the aid from seaward, and green if he is to the left of the desired track.

A typical example is the Thames River Upper Directional Light (Connecticut) that shows an isophase 6-second white light, over an arc of 3 degrees, with green and red sectors 3-degrees wide on either side; it cannot be seen from any other direction. A quite different light is the Kailua Bay Entrance Directional Light (Hawaii) that shows an occulting 4-second white light, 3-degrees wide on either side of the correct heading of 023 degrees True, with a green sector 34-degrees wide and a red sector 70 degrees in width.

Directional lights will normally have an occulting or isophase characteristic so that they are easily followed.

Caution Regarding Directional Lights

A skipper should not place too great reliance on the various colors of a directional light for safe positional information. As noted for light sectors, the boundaries between colors are not sharp and clear; the light shades imperceptibly from one color to the other along the stated, and charted, dividing lines.